Dr. Lutz Knoche

Luck is not a coincidence

Positive thinking is not enough

The book has been revised from the German original "Werde zum Schöpfer deines Leben" and translated into English by Shoaib Fayzi

AF221283

Herstellung und Verlag

BoD- Books on Demand, Norderstedt

ISBN 9783753442594

Author

Dr. Lutz Knoche worked for many years as a psychotherapist and coach. For several years he has started to write guides based on his knowledge and practical experience. In his books, he includes case studies from his practice and presents proven exercises for immediate help. In addition to classical psychology, he has developed therapeutic hypnosis and bioenergetics methods and applied them successfully. He worked with many people from all walks of life, with socially disadvantaged young people, couples, young entrepreneurs in success coaching, politicians, entrepreneurs, managers, and artists. Now he mainly wants to make his knowledge and experience accessible to many people through publications.

Dr. Lutz Knoche has asserted his right to be identified as the author of this Work accordance with the Copyright and Designs.

Luck is not a coincidence

Being an optimist is not enough

Contents

4

1 Introduction

Many people don't believe in coincidences. But if it's not a coincidence, what is it? Are we dealing here with the acts of a higher power? I think that we consciously but mainly unconsciously evoke these "coincidences", which are not accidental. It's a real process, if not entirely straightforward. No matter what goals or wishes you have, their fulfillment is always linked to cooperation with others. Only through many types of direct and indirect cooperation will you become who you are.

Please follow me:
You are not viable without cooperation with others. It is only when you start cooperating with others that you start to live. Right from or before your birth. How your life then goes depends solely on the type of cooperation you enter into. Offered to you in an infinite variety. So if you know what you want, all you have to do is look for the right collaborations. That is more difficult than I said. You have to describe your goals exactly, recognize which partnerships you have to enter into and how you can get them. Direct cooperation partners are people you meet personally. All products and services that you use are also direct cooperations with the manufacturers and service providers. In these cases, you just need to identify the right cooperation partner. But even that can be very difficult at times.

It is more important and even more difficult with the indirect ones. These are, for example, people who change a timetable. As a result, a guest arrives later than usual and that's the only reason they meet him. Who might be suitable cooperation or life partner for them? I.e. the person who changed the timetable has cooperated with you indirectly. You can influence both types of cooperation to achieve your goal, including indirect ones. There is a way to do this. I will introduce it to you in this book.

Successful people don't just use their minds to do this. Consciously, but mostly unconsciously, they mainly use their "subconscious". There, through thoughts and feelings, they create targeted, direct and indirect cooperation. At the same time, they weaken or eliminate disruptive and blocking collaborations. In this book, I will show you how you can create or change this through the use of your subconscious.

When you understand and master this, you will achieve anything you desire. Your heart's desires will come true. I will show you which mistakes are made again and again and explain step by step how you can successfully implement your wish.

Some of you have probably already dealt with wish-fulfillment methods. There are a large number of more or less scientifically promising approaches. There are many books on this, such as The Book of Secrets "by Deepak Chopra, which explains how one can fulfill one's dreams through faith and intense wishes. Similar books like, "The Power of Your Thoughts" by Erhard F. Freitag, "The Power of Your Subconscious" by Joseph Murphy, "The Seven Spiritual Laws of Success" by Deepak Chopra, etc., show ways to wish fulfillment. About the latter, I have written a small coaching book, "Coaching: The seven spiritual laws of success" according to Deepak Chopra in German and English as an e-book. It is very popular.

I assume that some of you have tried these methods before. But only with moderate success. There are really good methods that lead to wish fulfillment. You must create the right conditions, formulate your goals clearly and direct your thoughts and feelings towards the fulfillment of your wishes. There are sufficient scientific experiments and findings from a wide variety of areas that document the success of these methods. I will tell you about some of them.

In particle physics, for example, phenomena were discovered that have neither space nor time, i.e. cannot originate from the material world. Nevertheless, they were discovered with highly sensitive measuring devices. What kind of phenomena are these? Where do they come from when they are not in our material world? There is no proven explanation. Maybe they only become something through our thinking and filling, according to our ideas. As demonstrated experimentally in quantum physics,

So if not matter, then consciousness. If it cannot be in this form in our time and space-shaped consciousness, then in the universal consciousness. The universal consciousness has no time and no space, exactly what characterizes these discovered phenomena. This would mean that the material world is seamlessly connected to consciousness and that matter flows through it. The material world, including us, therefore consists not only of matter but also of universal consciousness. Both do not exist side by side, but as a whole within each other. These phenomena exist everywhere, including within us. So what has been seen as a divine spark in every human being for thousands of years is now understandable.

The further logical conclusion is that everyone is part of the universal consciousness. When we have recognized this and recognize how the connection between matter and consciousness works and for what purpose, then we have possibilities that we were not aware of until today. So there is a way in which we can create our life purposefully through thinking and feeling. You will receive detailed instructions for this. In connection with this, I would like to mention another proven phenomenon.

A groundbreaking discovery was made in neurological research. When we start to think about something, our brain starts to react for a fraction of a second. So before we even think of thinking about something. So impulses come independently of us and influence our thoughts and actions. They are believed to come from the subconscious. But why? What kind of impulses are these? Who or what initiates it, since we cannot be? But can we still influence you specifically? You will find an answer to all of these questions here.

I will describe many case studies and give detailed instructions on how to fulfill wishes. Everyone can just use it for themselves. But I don't want them to believe me because I am making them great promises. I want to convince them with my mind. In this way, wish-fulfillment becomes a complex process that is broken down and explained in detail in this book.

The removal of blockages is of great importance. They keep you from fulfilling your wishes again and again. These are beliefs, prejudices, doubts, disappointment, and much more. Self-hypnosis is an extremely effective method to counteract this.

It is simply undisputed that hypnosis is the strongest force in our "subconscious" that can release and dissolve blockages. But it can do more than just that. We can work with it in our "subconscious" and make positive changes. And that leads to new knowledge. A new door of consciousness opens. We enter a room that is still strange to us and opens up unimagined possibilities.

I'll tell you what I already know about this room. How and why events manifest in the future. Why then there is a high probability that wishes will come true. Science, quantum physics, and spirituality merge naturally and understandably. Once you allow it, you leave the material, performance-related, and market economy worldview. That, in turn, is the decisive step for the continued existence of humanity. Everyone has evolutionary instincts that allow them to recognize the truthfulness of a statement or an experience. Just let it happen.

You will learn everything you need to do to become the creator of your own life and what has kept you from doing it, despite the best of intentions.

There is universal consciousness. It is connected to each individual. With which you cooperate through your "subconscious" through your thoughts and feelings. I'll prove it to you. Everything is already there. It just needs to be put together. From this, we can recognize new things that are still unknown to our previous worldview. You, with your thoughts and feelings, are part of a whole and in the middle of it.

To creatively influence reality through your thoughts and feelings to make your wishes come true, is a new way, with high potential and many possibilities.

Findings that do not fit into our old worldview are initially ignored or rejected by many, despite countless verifiable experiments. In this case, it even takes us beyond our firmly anchored material view. That is particularly difficult to accept.

In this case, however, it affects each individual personally. Because immediately after reading this book, in your life, with the help of your thoughts and feelings, you can fulfill your wishes and lead a successful, happy, and fulfilled life. No matter how others think about it. It's up to you.

In many areas of psychology, medicine, physics, quantum physics, and other areas of science, puzzles have been recognized and proven experimentally. I already mentioned two of them in the preface. All you have to do is take these new steps and learn to implement them.

In this book, you will learn from my 20 years of practical experience how to logically and easily implement how you can get from all the knowledge to a higher level of consciousness. How you, as a person, can free yourself from your materially limited level of consciousness and specifically cooperate with other levels that advance you. This can help you to shape your life more positively in a completely new way. And, once you have understood and implemented it, you will save yourself a lot of time and achieve your goals faster. Your life will become more fulfilling and happier.

I wish you exciting reading while reading and good luck with the implementation.

2. Mind and Consciousness

The mind is usually equated with rational thinking. We gain personal experience and acquire knowledge from outside. We use this wealth of knowledge and experience to make hundreds of decisions every day. It creates self-confidence and our EGO. Everyone believes that they think correctly and act correctly for themselves. He or she is in their little EGO universe. However, this often encapsulates itself from new ideas and knowledge, but above all from the much smarter universal consciousness.

To put it humorously with my EGO: "Everyone makes mistakes, maybe I too."

Everything that is brought out of your mind is the sum of your knowledge and experiences and not the absolute truth. Then there are also your prejudices and beliefs. Nobody knows everything and has experienced everything, so that your opinions, your convictions, and decisions are only ever based on half-truths and personal correct and wrong beliefs.

We make decisions based on our knowledge and experience. If a decision has proven itself or has proven itself several times, it is saved as "correct" and retrieved again in similar situations.

The only questions are: Has it proven itself? What were the effects in the medium and long term? And if it has proven itself: then does it have to be correct in a similar situation and at a different time?

In my coaching, I ask these questions frequently and don't give up until they have been answered honestly. The result is most devastating. It turns out that in the imperfection of our own experiences and half-knowledge we are often not in a position to make correct decisions in the long term. Unfortunately, most people live by it today.

Or we believe one person more than the other. That can be right. But it can also be that who you believe can only speak well or manipulate. You can find a suitable example in election campaigns. Even in ancient Greece, democracy was built on speeches with false claims and promises as well as manipulation. Today it is perfected with all methods of technology and psychology. There are specialists for that. The question is permissible: "What are" democratic "elections worth?"

Wrong beliefs mean that people and situations are interpreted unrealistically. Thinking is activated incorrectly and consequently, leads to wrong actions. Changing these beliefs in turn only with the mind and rationally usually does not lead to a lasting positive change. They sit deep within us and are emotionally and emotionally bound. These forces are stronger than our minds. But there are solutions. I will explain this to you in the next few chapters.

Let me first discuss another phenomenon in this chapter.

Surely it has happened to you too. Your decision or behavior does not correspond to your sanity. You know very well that it is wrong to be afraid, for example. But you can't do anything about it. Despite EGO and understanding. Stronger forces are at work here that they allegedly cannot influence or can only handle with difficulty.

Where does this strong force come from?

It comes from your "subconscious". The "subconscious" is often compared to an iceberg. Whereby the upper part above the surface is called consciousness and the much larger lower part is called "subconscious". This comparison is suitable for illustration purposes.

If you stop at this explanation, the "subconscious" is seen as a hodgepodge of all experiences and emotions that we have stored there. Because the conscious mind did not think it necessary for us to remember or because we no longer want to remember, it has entered the subconscious. The latter leads to mental and emotional blockages. They unconsciously influence our feelings and thoughts. That in turn influences our actions. We can solve problems in the subconscious by dissolving blockages such as fears, low self-esteem, and much more. We can also change behavior by influencing the subconscious. In my experience, hypnosis does this work very well, which I have been using in my coaching for many years.

But our subconscious is much more complex. Let us take up the comparison with the iceberg:

The iceberg floating in the ocean is directly connected to the ocean water. The ocean and water exchange information with each other. But the water is also connected to others again, such as land, air, wind, sun, and much more. This is also the case with our subconscious. So it can get an inexhaustible source of information. Therefore, in the future, they will no longer let me write from the "subconscious". This creates a wrong impression. From now on I will write about depth consciousness.

Our deep consciousness is therefore not just a hodgepodge of our experiences, thoughts, and feelings that we just can no longer remember, but it is the connection to the universal consciousness. From there we can receive or send specific information. You only have to know-how. If we use it correctly, it leads to a real expansion of consciousness. Yes, even for the creative shaping of our reality. Thoughts, feelings, and the real world are directly connected and influence one another. There is enough irrefutable evidence for this, and I will describe some of them to you in this book. Recognizing and using this is an essential step for the development of people and each individual.

Our consciousness can do a lot more than we previously thought, and that has been known for ages. Whether it was the shamans in primitive society or privileged religious leaders, through all ages, as well as other mentally inclined people.

In "modern times" there are many comprehensible experiments that astonish us. In this context, I would like to describe only a few here.

About 20 years ago I read a book, which left me speechless. It explained an experiment by Cleve Backster with a lie detector. This was connected to a plant out of curiosity. When this one sheet was cut off, the lie detector knocked out. Now they wanted to repeat this process. But this time the detector already knocked out when you took the scissors from the table and had the thought of cutting off a sheet. In other words, the plant already showed a reaction at the much thought. This experiment was carried on now.

First, you went into the room next door and thought of going to the plant to cut off a leaf. Again she showed a reaction. Then it was thought to light the plant with a lighter. This time the reaction was even stronger just at the thought. The experiment later showed that even at great distances the plant reacted at the same time with the thought. With just the thought you could stress plants so much that they grew noticeably weaker than others. The plants also grew stronger if you showed them good thoughts and feelings. Some of you are probably familiar with this effect. After this experiment, countless other experiments were made with plants, even over a distance from Europe to America. They always reacted.

These experiments prove: "We can directly change the material world, in this case, the plants, with thoughts and feelings." And that doesn't only work with plants. I'll go into that in more detail in this book.

Another experiment took place with animals. For example, you wired a dog that had a strong bond with its owner. The aim was to measure the dog's physical reaction. The man said goodbye to his dog and drove off in the car. After 300km he turned and drove back. Immediately the dog's heartbeat changed. If he was lying quietly on the meadow beforehand, he became increasingly restless and ran to the fence more and more often until his master was there again.

I've seen it myself. I had a dog that was in the garden all day. My way to work was 20 minutes by car. I left my institute at very different times and went home. So it wasn't an internal clock that could tick inside him.

But my neighbors knew exactly when I was coming home because whenever I drove off, 20 minutes beforehand, he was standing at the fence and waiting for me. It went so far that a visit from me, with whom I had an appointment, came when I was not yet home. But my neighbor said to him: "He's coming soon. The dog has been sitting in front of the fence for a quarter of an hour ". I came five minutes later. I was an hour late because I had some important problems to resolve at the institute. For me, it was natural that my dog felt when I was coming and waiting for me. I had so much to do in my institute back then that I didn't give it much thought. Only when he died and was no longer waiting for me at the fence did it occur to me and I asked myself: "How could he always know that?"

People who have close contact with animals know such or similar situations and may now say that this is nothing new. But think about it: "What are the forces working for this?" And "Can we perhaps use these forces for a lot more in a targeted manner?" Yes, we can. More on that later.

Another example started in Australia. A horde of monkeys has been observed there for months. It was observed that a monkey accidentally fell a fruit into the river. The monkey quickly grabbed it and then ate it. The water had probably made it cleaner and tasted better to him. In any case, he always washed the fruit in the water before he ate them. Soon all the monkeys followed suit. But the unbelievable thing was that monkeys were observed by chance on an offshore island and they too suddenly washed their fruits in the water, although it was impossible for them to have direct contact with each other. For this purpose, further experiments were successfully carried out worldwide.

Here, too, the question: Which forces are at work? One speaks here of a field of consciousness that exists independently of time and space and with which we are all connected. Among other things, it is called the morphogenetic field according to Rupert Sheldrake. It shows us that we can exchange knowledge and information with this field of consciousness, regardless of space and time. I call this field universal consciousness because there is much more to it than just knowledge and information.

At this point, I leave it to your imagination to deduce what would be possible with it if we could use this field in a targeted manner. The possibility of wish-fulfillment described in this book can open a door for this.

Many of them have certainly already had the following experiences:

You deal intensively with solving a problem. Find whatever information you can about it. You are full of emotions and want to solve this problem, but you do not succeed. At some point, your head will smoke so much that you let go of it and postpone thinking about it to a later point in time, or you just have other things to do first. Without you thinking about it, the solution suddenly occurs to you. Most of the time it is also very simple or obvious and you think: "Why didn't I think of it earlier?"

This process is often explained by the fact that you got stuck and therefore no solution was found. But when you let go, it continued to work within us unconsciously and the solution was found. By whom? If you had no further information and you have already thought very hard about it, where did the solution come from? This sparking creative thought. Can that be brought about in a targeted manner?

In my coaching, I let such processes of finding solutions run in hypnosis. For example, a client records the problem in hypnosis and asks for a solution, which of course is very emotional. Then he leaves the problem and leaves the hypnosis full of trust and gratitude that the solution will be found. The success rate that the solution suddenly comes to him shortly is very high and cannot be explained by coincidence.

In quantum physics, too, countless experiments have been carried out in the last 15 years that show how consciousness can influence matter. Here mainly at the atomic level. Here, too, it has been proven that thoughts and feelings can directly influence matters. If we assume that everything, including us, is made up of atoms, then this only leads to the conclusion that our thoughts and feelings can influence the real world. Experiments have shown that our feelings have a particularly strong effect and bring about changes on the atomic and universal level of consciousness. Each one of us can specifically influence matters with our thoughts and especially with our feelings. That means changing our real world immediately. In this way, we can also influence other people who are not yet known to us and find the necessary "cooperation partners". And we certainly do it more or less unconsciously.

But maybe you have already experienced such situations. For example, you have an important appointment. Sit in your belly car and it won't start. That means a catastrophe for them. You utter a "prayer" full of emotion. "Please don't let me down now, start." The car starts and you reach your destination. Is it all just coincidence? The stronger your emotions are, i.e. the more you want the car to start, the sooner it works.

It was the same for me too. I loved my old BMW 316. Although it was already decrepit, I couldn't part with it. Yes, "man" just loves his car, in the end, it often doesn't start. With good persuasion, I always managed to get it to work. In this case, it was not the feeling of help out of need, but "true love". At some point that didn't help either and I sent him into a well-deserved retirement, to a collector. He was just surprised that the car was still running for so long. When I explained to him that I had magical powers, he soon said goodbye and took my car with him.

At this point, I leave it to the reader's imagination to deduce what would be possible with it if we could use this field in a targeted manner. The possibility of wish-fulfillment described in this book would only be one step. If it is not always a coincidence, which forces are at work and how can they be used in a targeted manner? Let me pick that up later in the book.

3. Understand feelings as the language of the soul

In advance, I would like to make it clear that it is not important what you understand by the soul.

In psychology, the soul is equated with the psyche and in religion, it is independent of the body and immortal. It is only important for us that the feelings always come from the soul/psyche and everyone agrees on that.

I assume an immortal soul. For me, this is not just a question of belief, but logic.

As demonstrated, everything is connected to universal consciousness. One exchanges ideas with one another are influenced and can influence. Nothing but nothing at all is lost in our universe. Only the energy state can change.

So if our body dies and goes into a different energy state, why should our soul (consciousness) be lost? It is already connected to the universal consciousness the whole time anyway and can influence matter itself. That would be illogical if it suddenly disappeared after our body died. The body is only a part of us. Rather, previous cooperation becomes a symbiosis with the universal consciousness, i.e. a higher form of existence.

Based on our rational thinking and the development of our oversized EGOS, fears, claims to power, corruption, fraud, environmental destruction and decadence arise. We can hear that on the news every day. It cries out for fundamental changes. Material thinking promotes rational thinking. Feelings and emotions are therefore often viewed as weaknesses. Instead of believing in one's feelings, they are rationally explained as unimportant or annoying, up to and including permanent self-lies and thus lead from one failure to another, both privately and professionally. Loneliness, behavior problems, fears, and addiction are often the result.

But only our feelings and emotions decide in our life whether we are or will be happy or unhappy. They show us the way to ourselves. Feelings are the language of our soul. And our soul doesn't lie.

If the feelings are recognized and perceived by our EGO without evaluating them, they show us the right solution to the current problem. But this language of the soul is often not recognized. The original feelings are evaluated and the ratio around. The result is often the wrong decision.

This knowledge is of fundamental importance if you want to successfully apply this method of goal and wish-fulfillment presented in the book.

Why do most people find it difficult to listen to their feelings?

On the one hand, there are negative emotions and feelings that you often have from childhood, often even in the prenatal phase, lugging around with you in-depth throughout your life, developing false beliefs from them, and influencing your thinking and acting.

On the other hand, there are norms and rules that you have learned in your family and your entire social environment since childhood, but which do not match your own emotions and feelings.

These rules and norms are so firmly anchored that you believe in their correctness. They fear exclusion or punishment if these rules are broken. In doing so, you do not notice that this is precisely the reason why yourself is being marginalized and that conflict and unhappiness arise as a result. Often there are defiant reactions that only make things worse. The feelings do somersaults and are therefore suppressed and the helpless, rational consciousness mindlessly takes over the lead. Then narcotics of all kinds are often used.

All because you do not recognize feelings and emotions or your EGO reinterprets and suppresses them.

Again: feelings are the language of your soul to make it strong and happy.

It is they who show the right way out of our soul in deep consciousness. In this book, I will show you how to recognize and accept that. How you rewrite wrong manifested feelings, from unprocessed experiences, in your deep consciousness.

I will also show you how you can release your emotional intelligence and use it privately and professionally.

The ratio shouldn't judge feelings, because it can't. Feelings are true and the way to find yourself. But the ratio plays another important role. It should find practical ways, without judging, so that we can live our feelings. When we realize this, we have found the key to a happy and fulfilling life.

Let me also describe a case study at this point. In advance, however, I would like to state that in my cases I often talk about extreme cases. Most of them cannot identify with this directly, but such cases show that even then there is still a way out.

So let me begin.

I met a man in a homeless shelter. He was 29 years old. I noticed him because he stood out from the others in all of his behavior. It was very neat and clean. We started talking and I found that he was very intelligent and had good manners. He did not drink or use drugs. So how could a man like that end up here?

He later told me that from years of drug abuse he was diagnosed with paranoid schizophrenia 3 years ago. Now he's clean. But he had lost his job and his apartment too. So now he is sitting here in the homeless dormitory. I met him there again and then I decided to coach him in my practice.

After we built enough trust, he told me about himself. An exciting and dramatic story that would fill an entire book. Therefore, unfortunately, only the essentials on our topic here. M. was on his own at the age of 15. On his journey across Germany, he met many different people. So he came to alcohol and drugs very early. Sexual debauchery with women and with men was also normal for him for a while. Finally, he ended up with a friend who was also very into smoking weed. There were often loud arguments there and he was unhappy in that relationship. This relationship also gave him a certain hold and recognition towards others. So he came to terms with his role for a while. But it only became more bearable for him through alcohol and drugs. He often couldn't take it long at home and sometimes roamed the city all night, drinking and taking drugs when they were offered to him. He wasn't so interested in women anymore. He did it with them now and then, but only to see if it still worked, as he told me. To do this, he went to gay bars more and more often and made acquaintances with men there. But he did not consider himself homosexual. He had a girlfriend at home.

Now it happened that he met a man he fell in love with. He wasn't aware of that at the beginning. He just noticed how happy and free he felt. When he realized why he became very scared. He didn't want to be gay.

Indeed, homosexuality is no longer a crime. Foreign ministers, mayors, and many other public figures have already openly acknowledged this. Nevertheless, being gay is still associated with many clichés and prejudices. The public eye then mostly only sees the exotic depictions, which are often used for amusement, especially in American films, and this is generalized. This is how prejudices arise. The many other homosexuals, who usually don't look at it at all and lead a completely normal life, are not taken into account.

Of course, the whole upbringing and social environment are also geared towards family and children. Beliefs develop which in turn consider such a relationship to be bad, at least if it affects you. It is also known through the media that in some cultures homosexuality is forbidden and demonized. All these feelings and thoughts go into the universal consciousness and come back to us. Often adolescents who feel this predisposition then have great internal problems with it at the beginning.

M. also found it very difficult, because on the one hand he was magically drawn to his friend and on the other hand he didn't want this relationship. His prejudices, fears, and the influence of his social environment had finally triumphed. He broke up with him. And since that was incredibly difficult for him too, he only saw a final line for himself. He cursed and insulted him in such a way that there was no turning back.

He went back into an unhappy relationship with his girlfriend. But now he realized how unhappy he was. He drank tons of alcohol and drugs again. This type of anesthesia became permanent. So he got mental problems. Since paranoid schizophrenia usually occurs in young men around the age of 25 as a result of high alcohol consumption and drugs, the diagnosis was made quickly. In my opinion, that was not the case in this case.

This friend was the great love of his life. At least that's what I could deduce from what he told me. Due to his fear and the pressure that came from his social environment, he defended himself with all his might against these feelings and brutally ended this love relationship. However, as already explained, feelings are the language of our soul. If your soul is hurt so much, then it can lead to mental/psychological problems. Then there was the alcohol and drugs that made things worse. These mental problems are curable, but not paranoid schizophrenia.

Through my holistic coaching, I clarified the problem with him, which was not easy. The creative fulfillment of wishes played an important and helpful role. Today he has a job and an apartment again. He is still holding back with his male acquaintances, although he is already making some.

Now it is clear to him what he did to his friend. He still has to process that. He doesn't dare to contact him again. If he is no longer in love with him and wants to be with him, which would not make sense, even with what has happened there. Especially since I have to assume that the other loved him too.

A man can fall in love with another man and then have a happy love affair with a woman or with both. Life is colorful and full of emotions. Just listen to your feelings.

Love is the strongest feeling in the universe. It gives us the most positive energies and makes our souls grow. Those who have already truly loved know the feeling of this change and have then often surpassed themselves. No matter who or what their love is aimed at. That's why they listen to their soul. Give and receive this love with gratitude. This is the strongest force for your creative wish fulfillment. Follow the feeling of love that speaks from your soul. No matter what your mind and EGO say about it. It is always the right path to a happy and fulfilling life. But if you turn against your love, then this strongest force will work against you and will always hurt your life. Even if they are or are already successful in business or profession, in the worst-case scenario they will become mentally ill.

Fulfilling your wish for a happy partnership will show you the right way. Although love is of course not limited to the life partner.

This example shows you what role the wrong re-evaluation of our feelings through our EGO and social norms can play. And that's not even the worst scenario.

Suicide and serious crime are also not excluded in these cases.

Feelings are the power with which you can create your own life. With which you can influence reality and shape it according to your wishes. It is therefore immensely important that you cultivate your feelings, strengthen positives and weaken negatives. Love, happiness, gratitude is there, among many others the most positive feelings. On the other hand, hatred, envy, sadness, and fear are to be avoided at all costs.

Feelings can be controlled consciously and understood as language. Our soul helps us in this. In the next chapters, I will explain to you how this works and what options we have for it.

4. What is preventing you from fulfilling your wishes?

Everyone strives for the fulfillment of their desires and wants to lead a happy and fulfilled life. Most have already tried and some are working very hard on it, but they don't seem to be quite succeeding. I got to know very, very many people in my coaching, but very few of them lead a happy and fulfilling life. Why is that?

It is always up to us. In this section, you will learn what thoughts, feelings, and actions can prevent you from fulfilling your wishes. I am sure that this or that will immediately sound familiar and will fall like scales from your eyes. This section is therefore of great importance to you if you want to finally become the creator of your own life.

4.1 The doubt

Doubt is the end of all wish-fulfillment processes. Only through absolute certainty, i.e. without any doubt, can you shape your future according to your ideas. Not only are your wishes, with all the positive emotions, perceived by the universal consciousness, but also your doubts. If you feel doubts, the universal consciousness will tell you, then first think about what you want before I set something in motion. Anyone who doubts has already lost. It's not about the statement: It won't work anyway, but also about statements, "Let's see if it works. Or maybe it will work. "But also statements: "You do it once when it works, then I'll do it too. "Which makes you feel skeptical from the start and doesn't work anyway because everyone has different conditions. So if someone else is successful, it doesn't have to work for you. Everyone is different and has to find their way.

All such thoughts, feelings, and actions prevent your success. Most of those who have tried a method of wish fulfillment through their thoughts and feelings fail at this first point - doubt.

It is very difficult not to doubt.

As a rule, if you want to fulfill your wishes, it is necessary to break new ground. But when you break out of the old ways, there will immediately be people who notice this and want to warn you about it and see doubts. Sometimes it is meant well, but it is very damaging for you. Protect yourself from that. It would be best if you are completely clear about your wishes in advance. We'll get to that in the next chapter.

You should also think carefully about whom you tell about your wishes and goals, so as not to encounter resistance from others in the first place.

It is not always easy not to let any doubts arise, especially when your wishes take a while to come true and you also experience setbacks. You then succumb to the thought that the others might have been right after all or you get into self-doubt. That's human. If you get into such a situation, immediately push that thought or feeling away. Think about your desires and how good you feel. Send positive wish energy into the universal consciousness again and feel trust and gratitude.

On this topic, I would like to report on two case studies from my coaching.

The case of P.

P. was a middle-aged woman when she came to me. She grew up in a middle-class family. Even as a child she liked to paint. Therefore, her heart desired to become a painter. Her parents rejected this profession and called it a jobless art. So she became a graphic artist. By starting a family and by her job, she was busy for a long time and quite content with her life. As the children grew up, however, she became increasingly dissatisfied with her job. She now had more time to herself and started painting again on the side. In doing so, she fulfilled her heart's desire and quickly found the first recognition in it. She became increasingly dissatisfied with her job and then gave it up to devote herself entirely to painting.

Her husband was dissatisfied with it and did not believe in her success. Her parents also doubted it.

Although she was very happy with the painting, there were more or fewer doubters in her immediate social circle. P. was a strong woman, but this situation did not leave her without a trace. Her initial outside approval waned and she became insecure. Maybe the others were right? But painting was still her great love and filled her with great joy.

Now she sought advice from me. What should she do?

I visualized your success and let you feel how good it feels to paint and to be successful. I made them feel how good it is to be recognized for their work. Then I asked you to build up this visualization and these feelings whenever you had doubts. I asked her to speak as little as possible to her husband and parents about this subject. Your son and two friends were behind your decision and were convinced of your talent, yes, and real fans. She should talk to them about her work. If possible, she should get in touch with other more well-known painters and communicate with them. She did that too. Although she told her husband about her work and her encounters with other like-minded people, she no longer allowed discussions about the meaning of her work. Over time, her husband accompanied her from time to time when she met painters and like-minded people. He got to know interesting people and felt that his wife was very well recognized in this group. His attitude gradually changed. P. then got more and more recognition from outside and sells the first pictures at a profit. What a small breakthrough for a painter.

P. can live well with and through her painting today. Now she visualizes the next stage. Your international recognition. I am convinced that she can do that too.

The case of F.

F. was a young man aged 25. He was adopted as a toddler and since the woman finally had two children of her own, he did not have a loving childhood. So he left his stepfather's house at the age of 16. His youth was also very chaotic. Eventually, he ended up with an older dominant woman with whom he had lived for three years.

F. was very bright and intelligent. However, due to his path in life, he had extremely little self-confidence and left all important decisions to his partner. He also drank a lot and since his partner was on drugs, he certainly did the same. Thanks to his intelligence and creativity, he has often had very good ideas for getting ahead in business. However, his partner didn't think much of him and repeatedly doubted him. Due to his lack of self-confidence, however, he was unable to respond and then gave up again at some point.

A person who experienced little or no affection and love in their childhood cannot develop their self-esteem. Even as a child he asked himself: "What did I do wrong?" Even as an adult, such a person will usually not be able to develop strong self-confidence and will repeatedly doubt himself. Therefore he will look for a strong partner. That can help him a lot. Especially when the other is helping them to become stronger themselves. In such cases, even such a troubled person can become a self-confident personality.

In the case of F., he had unfortunately found the completely wrong partner. It is then very difficult to become one's creator of one's desires. Indeed, it would be difficult for him to formulate his heart's desires clearly and unequivocally since they certainly have nothing to do with his partner. This then has the consequence that a dominant partner then immediately counteracts it in a variety of ways. That makes him insecure again and leads to self-doubt.

Or he simply adapts his goals, his living conditions with such a partner. But these are no longer dearest wishes. So they are subliminally doubtful from the start, do not reach universal consciousness, and do not lead to wish fulfillment.

But F. was tireless, like a stand-up man. He wanted to be successful. Now he had set his mind full of enthusiasm to become successful with network marketing.

The first thought that occurred to me was: "How can a person like that, an alcoholic who also takes drugs and has no self-confidence, be successful in network marketing?"

A business where 90% of the time you only encounter rejection and then at home with a woman who smokes weed every day and repeatedly doubted her success. Yes, he denied his decision-making quality and believed that he could not make decisions on his own. She is the strong woman in his life.

That was a real challenge for a successful coach. The only thing I could stick to was that F. could not be dissuaded from his success. He was convinced of it.

Since he could be very charming and very good-looking, he had no problem getting in touch with other people quickly. However, he usually ended up in her bed. In the end, however, he was unable to convince her of his business and was then disappointed. He told me his kindness is always misunderstood and felt completely innocent. He always saw himself as a sex victim. "Everyone just wanted sex from him". He said. Incredible! This young man was so low in self-esteem that he constantly doubted his feelings and did what others wanted.

So he began to have doubts as to whether he would be successful with network marketing. The constant know-it-all of his girlfriend, who always broke everything up and gave him wrong advice, did the rest. So he came to me and wanted to know how he can be successful in the network. What should I do?

What he should have changed was obvious, but certainly, he would not have been ready at this point. So I asked him why he wanted to do network marketing. He explained to me that it's just a jump start to make money. He also wanted to bring his partner into financial security. But then break up with her because he doesn't love her. He told her that too. Then later he would do very different things.

How naive was this person? Such a dominant partner would never let go of that but would do everything now to ensure that it remains unsuccessful. She would see doubts directly and covertly until he doubts it himself and gives up his plan.

In this way, of course, one cannot achieve anything in the universal consciousness. It wasn't a heartfelt wish of his after all. As described above, he had adjusted this wish depending on his partner. With this success, he also wanted to take better care of you. In the end, he even wanted to be successful in network marketing with her. It couldn't go well and was going in the completely wrong direction.

I asked him to write down for me what heart's desires and goals he had. He did that then and brought it with him the next time. And I can tell you that they were very good wishes. They had absolutely nothing to do with his partner and nothing to do with network marketing. So I focused him on his wishes and not on the temporary solution. I introduced him to it in detail and told him that it only works if he treats it as his matter. So never told anyone, including his partner, because I was justified in fear that doubts would then be sown again from the start.

He then no longer doubted that he would fulfill the desires of his heart. After a while, he got clean and found a steady job to become financially independent from this older, dominant woman. He then separated from the woman and is now in the process of focusing on his actual heart's desires and putting them into practice.

I've had a lot to do with alcohol and drug addicts for a while and I know how hard it is to break free from addiction. I also know from many cases how difficult it is to get rid of a person who has built up a strong dependency on himself. He went this development path out of himself by visualizing his desires. The universal consciousness gave him the impulses, the decision-making, and the strength for it. He will certainly have to let go of some of his past, which I will describe in the next section. But the biggest hurdles have been overcome and I believe he can do it.

Such a case is not necessarily typical, but it shows once again that even cases that appear hopeless through the application of creative wish fulfillment are successful. One just has to send out the true heart's desires unmistakably. In his case, it was doubts from outside and the wrong wishes that ultimately made him doubt himself and that kept him from success.

If you have doubts more and more often, double-check your goals. Is it your heart's desire? If so, then rephrase them clearly and unambiguously. Do not look for intermediate goals. You do not know whether these lead to your actual wish fulfillment. Leave it to the universal consciousness. It will show you the right way. As was the case with F.

So doubts do not lead to success. But even if you saw doubts in others, it leads to the fact that the universal consciousness does not accept our wishes, because it shows unbelief and an oversized EGO.

If you feel negative about someone for doing something that you think is wrong or stupid, change your mind. You thereby damage other people's wish fulfillment, which affects your wish fulfillment. No matter what others do, they always treat them with respect and love. Do not throw any doubts unless it will harm anyone. If you create an atmosphere of respect and harmony, you will get the same in return for your wishes and goals.

Keep yourself away from doubters, eternal pessimists, and sarcastic. Even the opinion of others about your personal goals and the fulfillment of your wishes, no matter how well-meant and seemingly constructive comes from someone else's ego and does not have to be right for them. Nobody can put themselves in the place of your heart's desires and everyone always bases their advice on their experiences. As described in the first section, this is only about a limited EGO that gives you advice. That doesn't have to be for you, and it may even turn out to be wrong. This applies to all areas of your life. All of this can raise doubts in you and prevent you from fulfilling your wishes. So do not let yourself be persuaded or influenced, at least concerning your wishes, otherwise, doubts will arise again and again.

Formulate your heart's desires and listen to your feelings. Nothing more and nothing less will make you forget your doubts and lead you to success. You will find out how to formulate the right wishes and what needs to be considered to make them come true.

Here is a summary again

1. Formulate your heart's desires specifically and unequivocally. Feel how good it feels when your wishes come true. This increases your certainty that it is the right way and that you will come true.

2. Hold back your wishes in public. It's your very own business. In this way, you also keep doubters away from you.

3. If you have to let others know about your wishes, then isolate yourself from doubt. Prepare yourself mentally for it to happen. Interrupt any other opinions that are making you doubt if they are being forced upon you.

4. Formulate your wishes as if they have already been granted and are grateful for them. Feel how good it feels when your wishes are true and feel deep gratitude. When I feel real gratitude, I no longer doubt my wish-fulfillment. What else should I be grateful for? This increases your certainty and does not leave you in doubt.

5. If success is a long time coming or if you are constantly attacked by doubters, doubts may arise in you too. Don't be alarmed by it, it is human and you will be forgiven. But as you notice, reverse the direction and see how good it feels when your wishes have come true. Feel gratitude.

6. Don't be in constant doubt and, above all, never say or think: It won't work after all. This is a definitive rejection of universal consciousness. By then you have already lost and can start over.

7. If you often have doubts, even without influencing others, then check your wishes. Is it your heart's desires? Did you make it unmistakable and clear? If not, correct them. But don't do this all the time.

If you adhere to these points, nothing can stop you from turning your heart's desires into reality with your creative thoughts and feelings. You will then build the right collaborations that will lead you to wish fulfillment. All you have to do is follow the instructions below and use the methods presented in this book.

4.2 Let go

Let go. Your sadness, your fears, your emotional pain, and all other negative feelings. Because as long as you have these thoughts and feelings, you send them out too. The universal consciousness makes no judgment. It only registers what you are sending out and it comes back to you. So don't be surprised if you keep getting into the same uncomfortable situations or falling for the same guy over and over again.

I know from my own life and as a coach that letting go can be very difficult. But it is necessary. When you let go you become aware of your Creator for the first time. It can feel very good.

Here, too, a case study from my coaching.

A good-looking woman in her prime came to my practice. After a detailed discussion, I discovered that she had all the prerequisites to be successful. But it wasn't. At least not at this point. For two and a half years she could do what she wanted, but there was no success. She was freelance and had to live on welfare. A highly intelligent and friendly woman who possessed all the virtues and qualities to let the universal consciousness implement her wishes creatively. She even mastered meditation without any problems. Why was this woman no longer successful?

The answer came in the second conversation. A. had met someone. Already at the first meeting, they both felt a great familiarity and sympathy. After a few weeks, they moved in together and had a very intense relationship. Assertions on the part of the other:

"She is the most important person he has ever met in his life."

"Your touch is so beautiful and intense that every sex he had before was nowhere near as nice."

"In this relationship, we will experience highs together like never before in life."

She told me all these assurances from the former partner and tears stood in her eyes.

For them, it was a sign of a unique kinship. They planned a life together and then this person abandoned her two and a half years ago. It happened suddenly and very badly. A. was profoundly insulted and hurt. Without even knowing why.

She explained it with fear on the part of her partner. Afraid of these strong feelings. "That's so stupid," she said and couldn't understand. She still believed that they belonged together and could have lived a uniquely happy and fulfilling life together. She said: "Both of our souls would have grown enormously."

Of course, souls can meet those who belong together in this life. If they manage to stay together, they will also live full and happy lives and grow. In this case, however, it was the case that the soul of her partner had not yet had any experience with love. Though overwhelming to him at first, these great feelings frightened him over time. His soul kept shouting: I want this person. I love this person. But these new overwhelming feelings scared him and then made him do just the opposite to finally lose that fear.

He was also not used to such close ties. So far he has always felt free and independent. That was now lost, even though it did just the opposite. At first, he could feel free, but he didn't realize that yet. So it happened that he then with all his might ends this relationship in evil.

I explained this to my client: "It was certainly the first true love he felt for you. You probably found each other because they belong together. But in the universe, there is not just one soul that belongs to another. That would be the purest Chaos if everyone is looking for a single soul that suits them. There are many other souls. "

They weren't together anymore. She thought about it every day. Sometimes she was sad, sometimes angry, and often she was worried about the other. Often when you get up or before you go to bed. So at a time when feelings and thoughts reach the universal consciousness best. While she could switch off and do other things at times, her former partner was present every day.

It was no longer surprising that A. was unsuccessful for so long. This nasty and hurtful separation has stolen so much energy from her for two and a half years. She missed it. Also, at the best of times, she sent sadness, anger, and worry to the universal consciousness, which of course kept coming back to her. A. had to let go.

With her constant thoughts and feelings, which she still has and sends out to this soul, she also influenced the other. With her feelings and thoughts, she didn't create any cooperation that would bring her further. In this way, it also blocks the other soul's way back to it again, if that were correct. She cannot influence whether this path leads to her again or not. She just has to trust the universe in this case. The right thing will happen for you.

I went into hypnosis with her, which she knew, and there came an encounter with the other soul.

She said the following sentences:

1. I forgive you.

2. I bless you.

3. I love you and let go.

To 1. Forgiveness comes first because this is the only way to let someone go. In other words, if I still have a grudge against someone who wronged me or made me angry or sad, then I will carry it around with me. I have to forgive the other and thus lose my negative feelings, which are only keeping me from my path to success.

To 2. With the blessing, one feels the power to be able to bless someone. You feel like a creator. That feels good. You don't have to be a believer to bless someone. You just have to do it. That is not a privilege of religion, anyone can do it. Everyone is a part of creation and can bless whoever they want.

So I bless you in the name of creation that we are both made of. Everything is interrelated. So when I bless you, I am blessing creation and myself. Feel the tremendous positive power behind it when you do it.

To 3. If you still love someone, then you should say that too and not lie. Nevertheless, you let go of the other and give them over to the universe. If the two belong together, then they can only find each other again once the other let's go. If they don't belong together, then you've let go, you feel free and are open to other people, including love.

After the hypnosis of letting go, this works if you then firmly enter the desire for a happy relationship into your heart's desires without thinking about anyone in particular. This gradually frees you from the pain of love that you carry within yourself.

A. is very successful again today. She doesn't have a new partner yet, but she's also no longer in love pain. She is sure to meet the right partner.

Although lovesickness after a breakup is quite normal and can even make us grow under certain circumstances, unprocessed lovesickness and separation can have a lasting negative impact on a person's life. It keeps us from a happy and fulfilling life and it can harm other people as well.

For example, a person who has not dealt with this grief can harm his partner in a new relationship and make them sad, but also negatively influence friends and much more. That is why I have a small but in my opinion important book on this topic under the title "Love sickness and Separation" published as an e-book.

Letting go is also about letting go of your guilt. Every person has also taken guilt in his or her life. Nobody is perfect. If you feel guilty, then you are sending false information and feelings. Even if you keep regretting it. That's noble of you, but it doesn't get you anywhere. It will also lead you to wrong beliefs and prejudices, which we will discuss in detail in the next few sections.

So let go. If there are things that are bothering you and there is still something you can correct, then go for it. If not, forgive yourself. Always remember, no one is perfect, so allow yourself to make mistakes. Learn from it and forgive yourself. Love and bless yourself and let go of everything that is bothering you.

Another process of releasing are the prejudices and negative beliefs. They are essential for that, whether they are successful in the sense of desire fulfillment or not. Especially if the fulfillment is already reserved for a silver tray and they are blind due to advantages and do not recognize it. In the next sections, we now consider this area of our consciousness.

But here again a summary

1. Check if there are still negative feelings from the past in them. You do not need negative feelings. They are in their past. But they live here and now and want to make aware and creatively design their future and let their heart wishes come true. So let go of all negative feelings.

2. Negative feelings are always associated with events and to persons. Loosen these by visualizing and apply the above method of releasing. Repeat it until you can and you have finally resolved it.

3. Especially in the case of separations after a relationship, it can be difficult to solve emotionally. Your mind will not solve this problem result in the method mentioned above and send your heart's desire for a happy and fulfilled partnership into universal awareness. Because that's really what you want. Do not imagine any concrete person.

4. If you have to blame yourself, then forgive yourself and let go. If you can do something or weaken there, then do it. But superior to whether that makes sense and cannot only bring more problems with it. Otherwise, forgive themselves, with the above method and learn from it. It is a human mistake to make mistakes.

5. Negative feelings do not always have to do with events or persons from the past. Sometimes it is just other people who adversely affect or manipulate them for certain other people or events. Check that and let go. It does not make it a bit happier and is just bad for you when you hear something like that.

6. When you release, as described, your wishes will be very faster with the help of the creative power of your thoughts and feelings. Yes, sometimes, many times faster.

4.3. prejudices

There are enough prejudices. Should I perform all case studies in which false prejudices play a role, then this book would include several volumes. False prejudices usually lead us to false beliefs, which then deeper into our consciousness and influence all our thinking and feeling. They lead us from the way to a happy life.

How is there any prejudice?
In our lives, we are constantly confronted with new people and situations. To be able to react, we use our experiences and supposed knowledge of others to quickly see through the situation. This allows us to react faster. That is often necessary. We cannot earn a lot of information every time in a new situation and then process. In the literature, you often call drawers to think.
So we think in drawers and that is necessary. Decisive but with what content, mentally like emotional, we fill these drawers. That can be positive as well as negative. If these drawers are filled once, then it's hard to change again. Prejudices are stored in our depth awareness, even if we no longer remember them. So we are unconsciously reacted with our prejudices. So we do not notice anymore that our feelings and decisions are shaped by prejudices. This has been demonstrated in many investigations.

But there are also prejudices which are quite aware of and we sometimes maintain properly. I have heard more often in my coaching: "I can live well with my prejudices. Why should I change something? "In this case, the negative prejudices also serve to enhance your egos. These people are also very receptive to the experiences and opinions of others who still support these prejudices. But that prevents them on their way to find the right collaborations to lead a fulfilled and happy life.

Such prejudices already move through the whole story of humanity. Especially when it comes to people and groups of people. An extreme but simple example is the former race separation in the USA. White poor day laborers or farmer whom it felt bad, but felt the "black" totally superior. This gave you a personal appreciation of your egos. So racial hatred could be fueled. But it led to the fact that they put so much energy into this "racial hatred", so for the fulfillment of their heart desires, which had absolutely nothing to do with the "black" population, usually not enough. Added to this was the debt to the own bad situation. But I wise others blame, then I do not need to do anything anymore to improve my situation. So they deceived themselves. That stops from the way of the wisher filling. So never seek blame with others through prejudices. They only make themselves small.

As already mentioned, these stories can be continued by the history of all humanity. Not the single person has become happier in life. Mostly prejudices are called targeted so that a few can realize their interests and goals. And that's still like that today. Do not be made to the ball of such people. Focus on your heart desires and you will quickly find that you will only be held through these prejudices to find your way in luck and fulfillment.

It is amazing how fast you can come to prejudices. One or two negative or positive experiences are sometimes sufficient and already generalized and reject. Or is positive from predominance. If a few matching opinions come from others, then it becomes universal and a belief. He then determines in deep awareness. With all the negative or wrong positive feelings that belong to it. But is this statement general? After closer consideration, in most cases not.

It is therefore important to round these drawers from time to time and to question themselves, whether the thoughts and emotions are still right. Especially if you realize that you will be on the way to you fulfill your own goals or take you much too much energy. So this drawer is helpful to you or blocks or blocks your target filling. Prejudices, negative such as positives they inhibit or block them damage them.

Case study by S.

In my practice came s... She was a very sympathetic young woman and wanted to build a good business. Concretely determined she had not yet. But our own business, she has always wanted. It's best to do something with health or beauty. But she had no own money. She did not have suitable training in the health sector either. But she did not want an employee relationship or retraining. So that was a pretty bad starting position. Her greatest trump was her motivation and her very sympathetic occurrence.

I asked her if she was already in shops that want to build the stores. There she could independently lead a branch. She told me that she already got an offer. She wanted her. You would have completely set up the branch in the beauty area and then always paid a share of your profits until it was paid. The only condition was that they have to relate the goods to the wholesale price from the sponsor. But that would be no problem, as these were good and asked. But the sponsor was a Turk and with Turks, she does not do business. They just cheat one anyway, she said.

I asked her where she knew that. What she answered that this is well known. She has heard it myself a Turk. He has to know it best. I asked them, "How many examples do you know personally, where Turks have cheated?" She just shrugged and said, I do not know now.

I have already met so many love and good Turks here in Berlin. Of course, that was a prejudice of her. I thought, "Hello, there will now send a heart's desire in-universe, then gets a positive answer and does not take that because she has this stupid advantage." Since the Turk already had some branches, I just asked her, In one or two or from me to go to everyone and talk to the operators, how working with him so. She did that too and got clear positive feedback.

With this information, you can go to me for the second time. She had already talked to the sponsor, so Turks and expressed her interest. I asked her if now her prejudice was eliminated. She said she was still skeptical.

Now skepticism is not bad in business with others that you do not yet know right. For inquiries from my side, but I realized that this skepticism still relies mainly upon because he is a Turk. According to my experiences about the wish for the wishes, she would not have received the business, and if, they cannot be successful.

I, therefore, asked you to know better. Also, I offered her if she keeps her attitude wrong, but emotionally has problems with a hypnosis session of this prejudice.

In the third session, she told me about the conversation with him and that they want to do a contract now. I advised her to check the contract, as with anyone else. Today she manages independently a branch and is successful.

What are the people who are exposed to the prejudices?

Some people have been exposed to prejudice since childhood. In children, this begins to manifest the fourth year of life into depth awareness. Often some people do not fit into the average picture of a social group. As you are too fat, you are too stupid, you are black, and much more. Over time, they believe in themselves and it fixes themselves in their depth consciousness. Become older, then control them and seek their way, even if they continue to expose prejudices. The prejudices and doubts for themselves in childhood are often unconscious. The process of creative wish filling is thus highly inhibited. As described in the section Doubt already described.

Let me report about two cases.

The case J.

J. came to my coaching to me. It was a 32-year-old man with dark skin and white hair. He spoke perfect German. That does not mean perfect but in the perfect Berlin dialect. He was born in Germany and lived here for his life. His mother was German and his father was from Namibia. He grew up with his mother and lived here in Berlin.

His concern was me, he wanted to be successful. He had only vague ideas. At first, he told me something about his life. As a child, he was bullied by some students at school, as he was black. Although he could do nothing concrete, then he had the feeling that teachers treat him differently than the rest of the classmates. A teacher, with whom he understood well, tells him, "You have to be better than the other, so you will find recognition." At that time he saw black musicians and actors who found high recognition. That became his role models. Songs, however, he could not discover any special great talents and was only mediocre at school. Even today he will be bubbled by strange people, just because he was black. He now feels like a failure and wanted to get out of this dead-end, as he said to me.

I asked J. if he already had experiences and success that made him happy. He answered that he always arrives well in women and had many women. Also, he had inherited his big link certainly from his father, which is also prejudiced on his part. "Most women drive off. But certainly, that helps me to successfully become successful in life, "he pushed quietly and thoughtfully. What he was right. But it was also human that he has focused on these successes as other successes previously. Unfortunately, because of his enthusiasm,

I put that he used much of his thoughts, feelings, and energies for it. Where was there enough room for his creative wish to fulfill?

In this case, several prejudices came to wear. On one thing, it was the prejudices of others who pulled him down. On the other hand, the one doubted that even prejudices have caused him.

Just because he is black, he has to bring a lot of good performance, which is a prejudice that was told him and what he has internalized. But since he was unable to do so, he felt like a failure. So because he looks different, he has to afford more to be equivalent to others. That's wrong! We are all parts of a whole and nobody has to prove his equivalence there. He does not have to do that if he wants to lead a happy and fulfilling life.

His appearance deviating from the rule came well only in women, so he focused that to find recognition. Although in a sense understandable but also wrong. He confined themselves and degraded himself on only this one thing because he held out more inwardly for nothing else. So he could not find or recognize the right cooperation to fulfill his wishes creatively.

I started with him with creative wishful fulfillment. He wrote me his heart wishes and after we had reformulated they were good. However, I had to ask if he does not wish for a fulfilled and happy partnership because that did not happen in his wishes.

He answered quickly: "Of course I wish that. I just forgot that. Is a matter of course for me? "

What happens to me more often with macho men? As for women or maybe men, they are sure of their thing. So why should you waste a wish for it? But it only meets what we wish for all of us. You can still think of so irresistible if you do not want a happy relationship, then you do not get them either. So you wish everything that your heart wishes are, otherwise no one, not even the universal consciousness.

We then went to the wish-fulfilling process, which he continues to date. His heart's desire for a creative profession has already been fulfilled. He works in resistance in the kitchen and is very gifted. He is estimated and is popular. He already has a festive girlfriend. Whether it's a big love, I do not know. If not then it certainly comes. So he is on the way to his heart wishes to fulfill. It will succeed, I'm sure.

Case F.
F. was a young girl and 19 years old. She was very pretty and friendly. Your concern was to be slimmer. I was amazed. To hypnosis, women often came and rarely men to me who wanted to lose weight. But those were people who very much fat content in the body had. Since, of course, a healthy body in the holistic

nature of body, mind, and soul is important, I also liked to help you.

V. had a strong physique and no fat, all proportions voted. A beautiful young woman. Where should she lose weight? She told me her story. Even as a child she was fat. Therefore, she was teased at school. When she got older, her mother said, she should do something for her figure and not eat so much. Her girlfriends also sometimes looked at them perceived. It was always very bad when she went to the bathroom with them. She likes to swim. But now she is no longer going swimming because she is ashamed. Now she has applied to two places as a bureau fish woman but was always rejected. She pushed it to be just too fat and thus unattractive. She was very desperate and wanted to lose weight now.

Through her strong physique, she was already in childhood, exposed to prejudice they were too fat. Later than she was a teenager, it was reinforced by her mother and friends. That sat down in her deep awareness and determines her thinking and her feelings. So she felt unattractive and beamed to the outside of course. Her self-confidence was therefore very low. Of course, that had an impact on your actions and application. Since she was really good and was very friendly, I could not imagine that it was at her appearance, why she did not get the place. Even its degree in vocational training was between good and very good. So she had all the conditions to be happy and successful.

Here I turned a trick. I explained to her that hypnosis only works with her if we involve her entire wishes she has. First of all, I would have to know why she wants to become slimmer. She had to write that back to me and of course, it already corresponded to her heart wishes of love, partnership, family, and professional success. We formulated these wishes correctly and built them into a creative wish fulfill. I still explained to her that these wishes are that they make me happy. Losing weight would be just a side effect if necessary to fulfill its actual wishes. It should therefore conclude the losing weight out of your wishes, but keep an eye on your heart wishes. The universal consciousness would already know how much you would have to lose weight. She did that and kept consistently to the desired program, which I gave her.

The next job interview was successful after 3 weeks, where she always wanted to work. She had also decreased by 3 kg. Although that was not great in her bodybuilding, she was so happy that she went swimming again. Then she learned to know her current friend. What lucky luck.

What about the wrong positive prejudice? For this example, about twenty years ago, the ideology of the good money of America also spilled over Europe.

Money is good, money is nice, and money is therefore desirable. There were also many books about how beautiful money is. Also, I remember a hypnosis cd: Money, money, money, a lot of money was suggested and there were many such CDs. Of course, the ideologically controlled. In a market economy, you need money. Money to buy all these meaningful but mostly pointless things so that the capitalist economy continues to flourish. As a result, doing a few, but they have the power of crowds worldwide to manipulate in such away.

After twenty years, our young generation has already reached and leaves traces. Sometimes you feel like it's all just about money. There are always better methods, of course, trained for a lot of money, as everyone can get more money. Even in social relationships and friendships, where it used to be taboo, it now takes more or less a place. Everyone wants to earn money as much as possible.

The money is good after everyone should strive is a prejudice. Like every prejudice, it sits in our depth awareness and unconsciously affects our thinking and feel. That makes some people ever dissatisfied and they do not know why. More and more people are therefore building "shops", where they want to inspire others from the family, friends, and acquaintances because they earn money through new employees.

Friendships, acquaintances, and family relationships are already broken.

Sometimes new acquaintances and friendships are purposefully built to win the confidence and then make new employees. This is very questionable in my view character and morally questionable. But that does not bother the one, the main thing they earn money with it. This is trained correctly and is not only limited to misunderstand network marketing but always pulls larger circles. More and more companies offer their customers lucrative bonuses when they win new customers. There are more and more fraud systems, especially through the Internet, which promise people for little money a lot of money, especially if they promote other customers. These are often very transparent fraud meshes, but there are always pure because they have become blind and only seeing money.

Another phenomenon is that people do not want to spend their money. Everything should be cheap for you or if possible free of charge. This is driving, especially in the country where I write this book flowers. I know millionaires who go to dinner in socially supported canteens, just to save money. Many successful wealthy people even haggle even at a very reasonable price to pay less.

Of course, you do not like to give away what you love yourself like money. This love for money is committed to more and more people in the deep awareness and affects thoughts and feelings unnoticed. This has nothing to do with the previously praised virtue of economy. It is a complete contradiction to further development and does not lead to the desired fulfillment, but more and more dissatisfaction.

You can see what a wrong avoidance can do with a positive prejudice. The heart's desire for prosperity is a good wish and certainly has something to do with money. But how they properly formulate this wish and install them in their heart desires so that he is true, learn. But with positive prejudices, it's not just about money. Other people who are avoidable successful can be hindrances to their wishes. So it is a prejudice that strong or successful people know how it works and can help them. Of course, this can make in a few cases, but in most not.

Be full of yourself with your creative wish fulfillment and do not rely on others. Especially if you mainly give you "wise" advice or note that you only exploit by turning it into the directions that are useful for the other. They alone know what is good for them and what way they have to go. They are shown the right way in fulfilling their heart wishes and only they can recognize him.

Therefore, are looking for, in this matter not your advice from others. From other people who avoid knowing better. Nobody knows their soul. They only know them and only with them can they let their wishes be true about the universal awareness. So you will find people who only do through them, without rating and evaluation, to help them consciously or unconsciously. It does not matter if these are now strong or successful. So set the prejudice that you can help you strong or successful people. Leave the universal awareness to create the right collaborations. You just have to recognize and accept them.

Prejudices, therefore, lead to them that if they do everything else right, the right intuitive information and merge from universal consciousness, but not recognizing them due to their prejudices. This will give you a chance for the other.

How can you change your prejudices?
From my coaching I know, it is not always easy to recognize his prejudices. Often they are already in our deep awareness, which keeps our minds and our ego correctly and sets them as knowledge. Avoidable knowledge to change is then very difficult. Therefore, they are reluctant and superior to what knowledge is based on their experiences or information and whether it can be generalized. Did you already have false decisions by personal opinions about people or

situations? Over time, you will recognize your prejudices. Listen to your inner votes.

If you have found prejudices, then they do not fight against it, but let them go. The method can be found in the chapter release. It may be that you now ask yourself: "Why should I love myself and bless before I let go of her?" Well, her prejudices were a long time a part of them. If you love yourself and are blessed, then everything to you. The universal consciousness makes no difference, whether it is right or wrong. That's why they stay and do not change this state. So you love and bless her prejudices but then let go. Only then will it succeed permanently and do not disturb your wish-fulfilling process.

Then program your prejudices. The reprogramming can be done as follows:

As described above, prejudices are stored in drawers in our depth awareness. Therefore, draw a cupboard with drawers. Write a prejudice on each drawer. Then write it around.

Examples from the stories:

Old: With Turks, you do not do business. The cheats only.

New: There are good and bad businessmen in Turks, like everywhere. I'm looking for the good ones.

Alt: For foreigners, you have to be careful. The ticks differently than me.

New: For foreigners, I can get to know new ways of life and cultures. This extends my knowledge and I can learn something for myself.

New: I'm unique like every person and have the power to fulfill my heart's wishes, no matter how I look.

So here again the same sentence. You can use that with every prejudice if you are even excluded for whatever reason.

Old: Money governs the world. It is therefore desirable to have a lot of money.

New: Money is neither good nor bad and for me only means for the purpose. Decisive is what I do with it.

Alt: Strong and successful people I take to the model because they know how to succeed.

New: Strong and successful people have done it and I am pleased for you. Also, I will create it from my power and with the right collaborations.

This enumeration could continue to continue. There are many prejudices. But I think the principle has become clear. Take a prejudice and always convert it with the goal of your wish fulfilled. Thus, not only dream of prejudices from their depth awareness, which they stop from their wish fulfilled. They even turn into the success-oriented direction and create the right collaborations. That's smart.

Summary

1. Prejudices arise through their own experiences that we generalize too quickly. Or through information and opinions from the outside, which we do not judge critically enough.

2. Prejudices are saved in our depth awareness, even if we do not remember them. So we often react unconsciously with our prejudice. It is therefore difficult to recognize and change them. But it is necessary to become happier.

3. Prejudices build you the way to the desired filling. They often do not recognize the opportunities given to them because they have prejudices. So do not judge your relationships with other people looking for appearance, age, or gender. These are benefits that can prevent your desired fulfillment. Just listen to your feelings.

4. If you are exposed to prejudices, you do not have to provide special services to be recognized. Set the following sentence in your depth consciousness: "I'm unique as every person and have the power to fulfill my heart's wishes." Feel this sentence. Be emotional and make him a strong belief in their depth awareness.

5. Prejudices are often ideologically, to achieve a few, spread and fueled. We make ourselves the game ball

of stakeholders. This considers us from our actual desired filling. Do not let that happen.

6. You alone know what is good for you and what way you have to go. You do not need to look for anyone who manages or looks after you. So be completely you in the process of your wish fulfillment.

7. If you have found prejudices, then do not fight against them, but let them go. The method can be found in the chapter release.

8. Program your prejudices. Take a prejudice and always convert it with the goal of your wish fulfilled. Be smart.

4.4. Belief

Often there is a seamless transition from prejudices to beliefs. However, beliefs are often addressed to themselves. How they assess themselves and their situation. It is no longer negative associations for beliefs, but deep emotional general imprints and beliefs. To interpret the world and act afterward we need beliefs. There are conducive and obstacle beliefs for your desired fulfillment.

Faith sentences are usually formed in childhood. At about 4 years we start to form beliefs. Certainly, there are many of childhood like:

You cannot do that, let me do that.

You will never get something from you.

You cannot do that, you are looking for something else,

You have to be diligent to get something out of yourself.

And much more.

Often such statements are unconsciously used by the parents. If you have children, pay attention to what they say and how they express themselves. Shape belongings like:

"You can do that" or:

"You can do everything you want".

You can therefore sustainably influence the life of your child more positively.

But also life situations in childhood can produce false beliefs. For example, the parents work a lot and have no time. From this, the faith can arise: I will not be loved. My parents do not want to be with me. I'm doing it all wrong.

Or they are teased at school because they may be too thick or have a dark skin color. From this the beliefs can arise: I am ugly. Nobody likes me.

They have difficulties in mathematics and are constantly criticized. They develop the beliefs: I'm too stupid. I cannot do it.

And so you can continue this. As a child, they cannot question such statements, but they suck them unfiltered and make themselves fast beliefs. Such beliefs are then in their depth awareness and influence their lives if they do not deliberately change something. Do not do it, then paralyze your actions and your cooperation ability. This can hold you from your wish fulfill. To convert negative beliefs into positive. If you are ready for it, it is easier than you believe

There are two difficulties:

1. You must first identify your false beliefs, as you often think of your thinking and feel, without you even aware of you, it is difficult for you to recognize you.

2. Conditions are not easy to change through the strong manifestation with their minds. So it's not easy as it cannot be changed solely on the direct path of our thinking. In this section, I show you how it works.

At this point a first case study

The case Y.
To me came to the coaching a young man. He was 26 years old and had a noticeable look. From outside he was a bit dark-skinned, had black hair, glowing eyes, and a sporty figure. He also seemed to be very intelligent. He told me he had a German mother and his father did not know. He was probably a dark-skinned American. Y. was born in Germany and he also grew up there. Through his external difference, he was already teased and marginalized as a child. His skin color and his dark hair were often referred to in other children as ugly. He also had the feeling that his mother did not like his appearance because she probably reminded him that too much of his father.
Although Y. noticed that he was attracting attention due to his good appearance with the women, he was

very shy, sometimes even blocked properly. Already through the experience of childhood, he had developed the fixed belief rate, he does not look good. He was dissatisfied with his appearance and had a lot to complain about what he described me to.

Here, how strong beliefs from childhood can distort the reflection of reality. Although he now remarked the opposite as a young man through the views and reactions of women, he firmly believed that he does not look good. So he was always looking for unobtrusive, not-so-attractive women who mostly lived at a low social level and also stood far below the intellect. He believed he did not earn anything better. He got to know attractive, intelligent women, then built himself in him, without he wanted it immediately a blockade and he finished contact. But he was very unfortunate himself.

Now the social status, appearance, and intelligence say nothing about the value of a person. I know that from my work. I have many people from social lower layers who had no good school education, which has proven to be very loving and valuable people.

In the creative wish fulfillment and so all people are the same.

In this case, it was different. He was unhappy. It was about the fulfillment of his heart's wishes, after a happy and fulfilled partnership. As the partner looked like and what intelligence degree they had to have, was not determined in this wish. Only he did not shout himself by his beliefs, he did not deserve anything else so that his wish is true. So my coaching did not start with the fact that he also dares to address pretty, intelligent women in the future, but thus to meet his heart's desire for a lucky relationship.

But first, he had to dissolve his belief from childhood. There are a variety of guidelines and methods as they change their beliefs and thus make a negative, positive. You can also try these. But if you use the process of creative desire fulfillment, you can easily convert your beliefs to their beliefs because they can immediately get in their depth consciousness and therefore can influence it permanently. So he had to let go.

In this case, all three levels were of great importance for him.

I love me.

He had to send that full of emotions to the universal consciousness. Through his false belief, he had very little self-love. Someone who does not love themselves has never experienced this love of others and cannot love others in full. How, if he has never made experiences with it. He has to realize that he is unique and valuable. He has to learn to love themselves. Convert their beliefs to:

"I am a valuable person and I'm worth giving love and receive love. I am grateful for that. "

I bless me.

He has to feel the force behind it in this sentence. He has the power of feeling itself and others blessed. He can be a creator. He decides his life and about what he holds of himself. He blesses. He is good and unique.

I let go.

Of course, with so little self-love, success and prosperity were also maintained. Since he did not recognize the necessary cooperation, even if they were served on the silver tray. Here he let go of these fateful beliefs. He lets him float up and see how he dissolves.

After that, he was able to succeed in his desire to fulfill.

In this example, two beliefs seemed mainly two beliefs that blocked the desired filling. On one thing: "I will not love" and on the other: "I am ugly."

In my coaching, I meet the belief sentence: "I will not love" very often. The approach of an explanation for this I have given them in the section "Understanding feelings as a language of the soul".

Imagine the questions:

Do you have the feeling of love? Do you love yourself? Do you give other people enough love?

In a negative answer, the following obstacles can build during their wishes:

Since they never experienced the feeling of love and therefore cannot love themselves, they do not even know what love is and how it feels. Often they scared them, this feeling that every person carries in themselves, so also in them. But they block and continue. As described in the first sentence in the book, there are no coincidences. Also encounters with other people both have produced themselves. Love is probably the most important feeling for a fulfilled and happy life. It's the right collaborations you make happy and continue. But if you are afraid and run away, you can let your wishes be bad.

Some feel very lonely and long for love that they have missed for so long. This cramps. They are very affectionate and possessive, in a person they want to have as a partner and who fell in love with them. This makes a happy relationship impossible. This permanent struggle for love and the separation pain that may not be tackled for her robs a lot of energy. That stops her with her wishful filling.

In this example, I showed them how to let go and convert this false belief into a positive one.

At this point another example.

In the section "Prejudices" I wrote about the love of money as a prejudice. But now there is the opposite, which harms our wishes as a belief rate. It is the rejection of the money. Faith sentences like: "Money spoils the character." Or "rich people live only at the expense of others" and so on, is also a false faith, which was also mostly influenced in childhood. It generates a dislike of money in our depth awareness, which is often no longer aware of us. Of course, that breaks us in the desire for the wishes, such as a worry-free life, lives in prosperity, or business success. Money is the abstract value of a performance, a thing, or a service. So money is neither good nor bad but only means for the purpose. How we deal with these values, that's a very different thing and will be explained later

Let me tell you a case study on this topic.

Case C.
C. was a middle-aged woman. She was an entrepreneur and a real "Super Woman". She told me she had already built three companies in her life. It was always very good at the beginning. She found recognition and had success. As an interior design, she had an advisory office at the beginning. After a good start, it ran very well for four years but suddenly worse again and she

had to close the office. But had already found something else and became a freelance employee as an industrial designer. That too went very well for four years and then it was over again. After that, she founded and led a school for design and had four employees. They did not just shoulder those skilled in the art but in most cases simple people who were interested in this area to make it possible to design their habitats. That was unique at that time and got along very well. Again, there were five years well. After that, she had to sign up for bankruptcy.

C. Just did not know why she always happens to keep the successes permanently. "I broke my head so often and just do not come to a statement," she said to me. Friends and relatives have thought about them. Some believed that it cannot be done with the right things. She should go to a shaman. That did it out of despair. And behold, the shaman found that a curse lies on her. Since she could imagine immediately, of whom the curse comes, she believed him and was astonished as he could find that. The curse was taken from her now and she was optimistic that everything is going well.

Let me explain a lot. Many people who use such services are confronted with one or the same multiple times. Each person has also experienced depths in his life, which he cannot explain. Sometimes a curse is just right and seems credible. Finally, there is an explanation for this. It creates an added value for the customer because the curse is taken one and one is grateful. Often he is still told him, he should come from time to time to be sure that the curse does not come back to him. So you then build yourself a customer base.

The universal consciousness cannot realize any wishes, which is directed against another man. Alone, because everyone has his free will and can decide which cooperation he goes on for his wishful and which is not. So if you experience a deep, then you have made false decisions and have received bad cooperation. This is based mainly on beliefs that you do not always have to be aware of. So not on negative influences or curses from the outside.

Surely some people have greater access to universal consciousness than currently most. Recognizing curses and take certainly not.

C. was firmly convinced that she has taken the shaman the curse and everything would be better. And behold, it went uphill again. She got a fixed freelance activity, a lot of money was not left with her bankruptcy. She also got a good affordable apartment despite its limiting financial possibilities. The work made her a lot of fun. That went well for two years and then she lost her activity and had to live on social services. Maybe it was wrong not to go to the shamans more often? But before she wanted to do that, she came to me first and wanted to know if I can help her.

After a detailed conversation, I quickly realized what it was that she had no permanent success. Since she was an entrepreneur and self-employed, the language of course came to the topic of money. It was so obvious what was the disturbing belief. She did not keep anything from money and certainly not of wealth.

From this belief, she derived her corporate governance:

1. "I always had moderate prices for my services. I do not want to draw the people from their pocket and become rich in their expense. But I could live well through a lot of work. More is not necessary. "

In my opinion, she sold her performance far below the value.

2. "I always had so much money as I need. That's enough for me. If I had more, I also liked spending it. Money must flow. "

In my opinion, she had such a dislike of having money that she did not want to have it with him and has spent it quickly for himself or others. She had not thought of necessary reserves in a self-employed activity.

3. "I have always given my surplus in social institutions, such as the children's house in place."

In my opinion, it was more or less her guilty conscience that she had when she earned more money more.

Of course, one could not be permanently successful with such a setting to the money as a self-employed. That was completely clear but she had not recognized it despite years of pondering. This belief was too firmly anchored in her.

I then led the following conversation:

What can this successful woman do everything well if you convert your belief to the right ones? That's what I said.

In the beginning, of course, the "Why Questions" was again:

Why is wealth bad? Answer: "Because money spoils the character."

Why does money spoil the character? Answer: "Because people can increase with others and think they are better than others."

Why do they do that? Answer: "Because you can afford more than others."

Why is that bad? Answer: "Because all people have the same right to live well."

Why should everyone live well, where they have different conditions and can afford one more and the other less? Answer: "For this, the individual cannot do anything. Nevertheless, it is just as valuable how one can afford more. "

After that I continued the solution interview:

How can that work? Answer: "If everyone can afford more, there is something of themselves."

So that works, it would not be right if they can afford more to do that too to support others? Answer: "Yes exactly."

Why do not they do that? Answer: "I've always done that!"

Do you have that? The more money you earn through your performance, the better you can do for others who cannot provide such high performance. Is that right? Answer: "Yes."

They have sold their achievements under the value and could not earn optimally money. Just because you have a negative attitude to money. But they could have supported much more. As a result, they have always lived on the limit of profitability. No company only runs well. So you need reserves. But they are even completely unusual, instead of bringing the high performance they can bring into the community. But their goal must be so much money as possible with their achievements, all the more useful are they too for others. Do you see that? Answer: "Yes".

You have also personally only lived on the edge of the cost of living. Just because you find money bad and ashamed if you own a lot of money, you have spent it quickly. But only if you are well financially good and you have built a stable safety, you can do optimally and permanently something for others. Is that right? Answer: "Yes."

What has brought you to these false acts, which then always led to deep blows? Answer: "My dislike for the money."

I agree. So get as much money as possible, so you get from your performance from the added value you create. Money is neither bad nor good. It only depends on how to use it. Do you recognize that now? Answer: "Yes."

Do you want to earn as much money as possible now and live yourself in a stable good financial situation so that you can optimally work for the general public? Answer: "Yes, I want that."

So we go now to let go of the old belief. We then went to let go: I love me, I bless me, I let go of the old faith. After that, we formulated a new faith and made him straight to a heart's request, which we sent to the universal consciousness:

"Money is, go bad. He will be fine if I take advantage of it. I would therefore like to be a lot of money and be rich. So I can and I want to introduce myself optimally to the whole and the general public. "

C. has built up a successful company after her bankruptcy and has already over thirty employees. So has created over 30 jobs through their ideas and strength. By the way, she just builds a house with six social housing. It supports some social institutions.

Private she bought a house, in one place where she feels comfortable and creating new power. Also financially she has secured. This is especially important in an experienced bankruptcy, otherwise fears that would only rob its energy.

I never doubted that she creates it.

For C. it was the right heart's request. But not everyone feels or thinks like them solitarily. This is not necessary as long as you do not think egoist. Besides, we will come later in the chapter "Set the right personal wishes."

What beliefs do you keep from your wish fulfill and what do you help?

To give you support I would like to enumerate some general approaches of beliefs. Of course, you can only serve as examples and are not complete. There are simply too many and they are dependent on each of them and what they have experienced. But I call them the most common approaches that lead to inhibiting beliefs. Delay or prevent your desired filling.

The first faith begins: I cannot do that because ......

I'm not smart enough and have a low school education, too little experience, have already tried everything and it did not work out, I'm sick, I know too little, and so on, and so on.

This belief: I cannot do that, arises, like most, already in childhood. She sits deep in us and is often unnoticed by us. But sometimes only to leave his comfort zone. So go back to the questions why I cannot do that and what can I change so I can do it. I want to change it. If I want to change it, then I can do it too.

Change your beliefs:

"I can do everything if I want."

If you do not want to create it then it does not belong to your heart's desires. To formulate your heart wishes and "want to" implement them too. Do not doubt her in which she says from the outset: "I cannot do that."

An example of my coaching

A young woman came to me. She was already 2 years unemployed and 32 years old. She had a dog there. At home, she had two dogs two cats, and still all sorts of small animals. She loves animals, she told me. She has also worked aid about the employment office in a zoo. That's a lot of fun. Unfortunately, there was no workplace in the long run for you. After a longer entertainment, she should tell me what your heart's desire is. She answered, preferably, I would be an animalist or veterinarian but I never can do that. I gave her the impulse to consider whether she wants to become an animal practitioner. Also there the answer came, but already with my secondary school cannot be done. Now training as an animal healing practitioner does not require a certain degree of school, I told her, and so it could make it out of home in distance learning. She gained the sample teaching books and the training content and it was exactly what she wanted.

Now I went to the wishful filling with her, which no longer has a doubt. She started her distance learning. After two years she was finished and had to conclude in an internship to a veterinarian she sought himself. She found that and made the three-month internship with him. Afterward, she got the offer to work at the vet as an assistant. Which of course they liked. She has been working there for almost two years now and now wants to build her animal healing practice in cooperation with the veterinarian.

From one: "I do not do it." It's an "I manage everything I want" and could successfully realize the wishful filling. She had the strength to complete her studies and found the right vet, which certainly was no coincidence.

The second faith begins: "Soon everything is better and easier, if... I first found a new apartment if I have completed my education if I made my driving license if I live in Berlin only." And so on, And so on.

So at some point, I'll live better. Its life or position to improve will simply be moved to a later date. After twenty years, they look back and festively have not yet become better. But it will never be a little better if you do not implement your ideas and wishes with your action in reality. Do something new is always with changes, do even with big changes, connected. Are you free for change? Moving to a later time, it always stops from your wish fulfill.

An example of my private circle of friends

It is always a problem in the circle of friends. On the one hand, I do not want to be a coach there, but also just have someone where I can lean on or do it, and on the other hand, the prophet is not much in his own house anyway. So helpful tips are neither wanted by me nor friends. Although of course, I can also be a good listener.

Now I had a friend who was very active to build his own business. But he also had a girlfriend who always advises him. Either immediately or at a later date, if it did not work right away. Then came: "I told you that right away. That does not work. "Everything he wanted to do, she was the doubt in person. He heard her and then began a short time full of enthusiasm for something new. If I did one first, then the other comes quite alone, he often said. He has not noticed for a long time that the first did not work. He did not understand why. Despite his commitment to me, that it is not a real love with his girlfriend, he pushed my careful remarks why he never succeeds, clearly side.

Now he wrote to me that he had spoken out of his girlfriend and want to separate. But since they could not afford two apartments for financial reasons, they continue to live together. However, in the four years in which they live together, their financial situation had never improved. Now two years have passed and they still live together. Their financial situation has become even worse and he will continue to succeed. In this case, he has installed several heart wishes. A happy relationship. Be successful and live in prosperity. A happy and fulfilled life, which he could have and can still have, is not possible.

If you realize what you keep from your heart's desire filling, then change it. You can always, at any time and immediately begin to complete it as soon as possible and bring about necessary changes. You just have to do it. Maybe leave your comfort zone.

Change this belief:

"It will never be a little better alone. Only I can do something better with my action and become better. "

Changes are always associated with they leave old or leave behind. Not everything was bad and she has made it more or less comfortable there in a way. That is not always so easy to leave something. You also have to change and get better. The first step would be to stop finding excuses why they cannot change now but finally come into action. Then they will be better because their old unsatisfied situation has certainly been very limited.

Feel: How do I feel, if I leave that behind me? Feel free and happy, then you should do it now. The feelings always show you the right way.

The third belief sentence begins with: I have to

...... go to work, save on a car, go to the cinema, and so on, and so on.

Also, they know from childhood. You must do your homework. You have to be better in school. You have to go to sport and much more. You usually have only been taught what you need to do in your life. You always make yourself the victim of your circumstances. Start rethinking. Ask yourself, I have to do that, which does not like me. Can I change or convert it into something that I like?

It is not always possible. Some obligations have to be made easy, even if you do not necessarily like it. But they will quickly realize that there are things that you just do so because you think, "I have to." But it is not that way. Sometimes they have just found themselves with the situation as they have been entered since their childhood. But that means standstill. In principle, they do not live in this world to do things, but to do things that they liked and who make them happy. This will make it succeed and advance the whole. This is the source of development and not what you have to do constantly and do not like to do.

Sometimes it's easy to attend your attitude to what you do. They say, "I have to go to work," but like to work. So say, "I want to go to work." Thus you change the feelings and the energies. You will probably be more successful. If you do not like going to work, you should consider whether you can change something. For example, by changing. All you with, I have to transform into one I want to transform it. So they do not feel more than victims but as a maker. So change your life and your feelings. It leads you faster to your wish fulfillment.

So change this belief in: "I want ... .."

Thus, you will be your life and judge her thinking and always feel more and more often what you want.

The fourth belief begins: "I have no time because

... .. I have so much to do. After all, I have to do important things. After all, I have to take care of my sick mother because I have so many dates and so on, and so on.

This belief has greatly developed strongly recently. In our present time, it has almost become a culture to always tell how little time you have or that you have no time. We live in a "no time society". This belief is already developing in childhood. If you are experiencing as a child that your parents have little time for them because they always have something else more important to do, this belief is also shaping them with them.

No time to have gradually becomes a lifestyle. Imagine, you want an appointment with anyone or someone who wants an appointment with them.

It has usually become a ritual, first of all, the difficulty to agree to make an appointment at all, urgently clarify. Mostly or then give or give the appointment with the reply: "If what comes in between, then I have your phone number and can call them".

No time to have "hip". Those who have no time are important and someone's time has the impression he is not busy or lazy. So more and more people are permanently under time pressure because they want to play an important role.

But do you use the time right? Hardly likely! Often they lose the look for the essentials. This is becoming a solid belief rate and is often implemented unnoticed. Thus, they often take the opportunity to recognize and accept the necessary indoor cooperation that help you with the wisher's fulfillment.

It is not about important appointments that must be met. But also there check if you have put the dates themselves and whether that is not different. So plan your appointments correctly or do not unconsciously sit down even under time pressure without it being necessary. This happens more frequently with my clients. Recognize what you really want to achieve and then focus on the essentials.

The essence lives departure and slowness. Through hustle and bustle, multifunctional ability, and indispensability, the look is often blocked. Once again, it's about to lose sight of the essentials and consistently work on the fulfillment of their heart desires.

In my book "Self-help with ADHD for teenagers and adults" I introduce a speed planning

So change this faith in: "I determine myself about my time and have always enough for my luck and fulfillment of my wishes."

How to use the time given to you in this life for the implementation of your wishes. Allows your soul optimally to grow and strengthens the whole universal consciousness. That's exactly what makes the meaning of life. Recognize that and internalize it.

Summary

1. To interpret and act the world we need beliefs. Some beliefs help us to fulfill our wishes and prevent us from it.

2. Faith sentences are usually shaped in childhood and then determine, often without us who is still aware of all our thinking and acting.

3. Through beliefs, we interpret the world subjectively. Everyone has his own beliefs and therefore sees the world with his eyes. Everyone is in principle convinced of the correctness of his interpretation.

4. Do not discuss with others if he in their opinion has a false belief. This is wasted energy and applies only to resistance. Thus, this belief in the other is only increasing. Everyone has to be ready to ask his beliefs in question and come to the realization to change something.

5. There are helpful and obstacle beliefs to fulfill our heart wishes. They are manifested in our depth consciousness. Indelible beliefs to recognize are therefore not easy, but it is necessary and possible to fulfill our wishes.

6. All beliefs that are a hindrance to our self-realization and restrict our self-determination are wrong. You can analyze and recognize that.

7. Faith sentences can be changed if you recognize them as a hindrance or wrong. It can be converted into conducive beliefs. Important is the conviction and the feeling that he is correct.

8. Commence beliefs create more space for necessary cooperation that enable us to fill us.

9. Commence beliefs lead us to self-determination and thus for self-realization.

5. Holistic recognition

It is enormously useful to make your wishes real as soon as possible if you go holistically to your desired fulfillment.

We have a body, in or with that we live. We think and are aware of us. We have feelings that explain how to come from our soul. We have a deep awareness, which influences our thoughts and feelings unconsciously and we are part of universal consciousness. Every five are connected directly to each other and influence us and us. They form a whole.

Think

The idea is influenced by our imperfect mind, but it exists independently of it. Every action, everything we do, springs from a thought that we have previously thought. Everything we think can also be real. Or vice versa, what I do not think will not be real either. With her thinking, she sets out specifically in motion and effect changes. Or they only believe but do not trade.

Often you hear the saying, you act before you think. Which is not right. Meant with that, you do not think before you are. That is, the thought is there before, but in this case, will not ask if he is correct or wrong. Sometimes it is also essential not to think about, for example in dangerous situations.

So we can ask questions or questions. This allows us to consciously influence our thoughts before we act. We yourself have it in your hand, what we do. It is our free will, as we think about a situation and whether we or what we do after. Although feelings, prejudices, doubts, beliefs, believe our thinking unconsciously influenced, we still have the free will to question our thoughts to make the best decision to trade. The thoughts are the fruits of our free will. From our thinking out, we can start to start changing feelings, doubts, prejudices, and beliefs. Thus, we even change our brain and create new neural connections that make us the right thing, in the sense of desire to fulfill, better. The more positive feelings and beliefs we have and so fewer doubts and negative prejudices, the better we can think. Everything is connected directly to each other. Only so we can successfully start our wishful filling. That's the foundation that makes us created with our free will.

An example of the desired filling:

I think: "I cannot change anyway because I'm sick, weak, etc. or because the world is just bad," then I will not think anything else. But what I do not think, do not act. I will never change something positive in my life

I think: "I can achieve everything I want." Then my thoughts and all other four, so the feelings, the body (including the brain), the deep awareness and the universal awareness then focus and I can lucky and I can happily and Fulfill form.

Body

But out of our thinking out of action, thereby changing things and developing things, but we can only use our body or our material physicality. Our body uses what we think and only the world can be changed. This is the meaning of the material world and life in her. Without the body, neither thought, feelings, the deep awareness is even changing or developing the universal consciousness of anything. The material physicality and consciousness are each other. Thoughts, feelings, and consciousness need the body to be able to work at all, so there. Only through the material world, including our physicality, thoughts and feelings can be lived and thus contribute to the growth of universal consciousness.

The body itself is a blank shell alone and is filled with thinking, feelings, with the work of our depth consciousness and the impulses from universal consciousness. It is logical that all influence each other to implement creative strength.

A healthy strong body can optimally implement creative concepts and the body can work better with a strong soul. Both are against the suit and counteract with each other. Our thinking then controls it and makes us act.

Two examples:

Example one

After countless proven spontaneous heals today every doctor is aware that the will to be healthy plays a major role in the healing process.

How does it come to such spontaneous healing?

First of all, the thought is: "I want to be healthy." Then the feelings are activated. The stronger they are, the greater the effect. This focuses the depth consciousness to exploit all possibilities in it. Finally, the universal awareness of healing is then set and creates the necessary cooperation for it. As the creator of the best external conditions, which always takes place through cooperation with other people, the contact with the right people who support me with my desire for thought through thoughts and feelings, contact to the doctor, etc.

So it can then come to spontaneous healing and the body can in the sense of the other four, further creative implementation.

Example two

All emotional events that have agreed in the memory of the depth consciousness uncoupled, also affect our body. You can build energetic blockages in your body and also lead to different physical complaints.

All mental traumatic events and feelings, which, for example, fears, self-confidential disorders u.V.M. manifest themselves physically. There are psychosomatic disorders, of which more and more people are affected. But they are not always recognized.

If you are recognized, then you can fix yourself. Previous Law is due to initial misdiagnosis and the drugs administered with their side effects, not otherwise damaged.

How can this be resolved?

On the one hand, the causes must be resolved. Often these are mental issues that are anchored in deep awareness. In this case, hypnosis is the first choice according to my experiences. She dissolves right there where the causes are also. In my coaching, where I also use hypnosis, that has already proven hundredfold.

On the other hand, the energetic blockages, which have manifested over time in the body, must be dissolved. Especially for this, I developed bioenergetics massage 20 years ago. Namely, I had found that the resolutions of the emotional causes do not have a sustainable effect, if not physically blocking.

I have turned in a video for this bioenergetics massage. This is on my HP: www.stressfreshein.de commercially available. After that, all can, whether professionally or just for themselves and their loved ones, can apply this special massage. Since everyone always builds new energetic blockages that do not always have to cause psychosomatic disorders, this massage is also very well used for the desired fulfillment process.

Feelings

About feelings have been written very much in this book. Feelings are very strong on all other four aspects of holistic. You can cause or solve mental problems. They affect our body and their charisma.

Feelings are the universal language between all levels, thinking, body, depth awareness, and universal consciousness. If this language would not exist, there is no cooperation between them. So no creative results. If this language is disturbed or is not understood correctly, then it comes to big problems. Since feelings are a language, the other levels cannot take direct influence on them. You can only understand them and act afterward or not.

Feelings are often evaluated and reinterpreted by our thinking. Often, prejudices and beliefs are responsible. This then leads to misunderstandings and wrong assessments. The consequence of it is wrong actions, incorrect information to the universal consciousness, physical blockages. In severe cases, negative manifestations in deep awareness and mental illnesses. It is therefore very important that you learn to understand and trust your feelings. If you control that, then you are free to fulfill your heart's wishes, for a happy and fulfilling life. Learn to understand this language and you will communicate with all levels and come much faster to your desired fulfillment.

How can I better understand this language?

A method that I successfully use in my coaching is the mirror method:

Imagine a mirror and look deep into the eyes, down to your soul. The eyes are the mirror of the soul. Think of the situation you want to solve, listen to your inner voice (feelings). At that moment your soul will give you the right answer. Hold this answer. Do not rate them. If you consider with your thoughts of this feeling and therefore want to change, why? Ask yourself, why? They then come across their false beliefs and prejudices. That's the first step to change something. The first feeling was the right one. You cannot change feelings. You can only evaluate them and keep them subjective for good or less good or bad. You cannot listen to feelings and make them numb. You can displace them, but they cannot change them. They are still there.

Practice this method again and again until you master it. The feelings come from our soul and the universal consciousness. There is no greater truth and no higher intelligence than this. Over time, they become more and more common, even without mirrors, to understand the language of their feelings.

Deep awareness

As explained in this book, her deep awareness is a powerful strength that influences her thinking and feeling but also her body. It is often has unrecognized in our consciousness. Deep awareness is far more than just the memory of all experiences and feelings that we have had in our life and stored there because we did not want them anymore. This is probably just a small part of what our deep awareness can do.

Our depth awareness can rather collect information that has not been stored by us. It can get information beyond your existence level and send your wishes. Wishes belonging to the universal consciousness and can become reality.

That clinks for most summarizes too fantastic but is completely understandable and normal if you capture the holistic. But that does not necessarily have to be successful. In this book, you will learn the technique and conditions for successfully going to your desired performance. But it can help you make your wishes come true faster if you understand the holistic.

So if you want to know more, I recommend that, the even indisputable masterpiece of Joseph Murphy "the power of your subconscious". Here you will learn everything about the great mechanisms and possibilities of your subconscious. In my book, I do not want to go further. It would only be a repetition, formulated differently. Many books have already been written on this topic afterward. But I would rather target them, because of my many years of practical experience, show how they bring their heart wishes into reality and what they need to pay attention to. Depth awareness is the key to contact with a higher dimension of our existence.

How can I use my depth consciousness for my wishful filling?

Above her deep awareness is like a bell, her rational consciousness on which her thinking is bound. To get into the deep awareness you have to deal with rational thinking. There are many methods such as meditation, yoga, affirmation, and much more. According to my personal experiences and experiences with clients, hypnosis is the most effective method.

For affirmations, aware of statements that have not yet arrived and said again and again, how: I am rich. I have a happy relationship, etc. That must come over with full conviction, which has many problems. But only then feelings are caused, which reach the universal consciousness. The other methods, except for the dynamic meditation, are aligned on relaxation.

In hypnosis, feelings can be conducted much more power directly to the universal consciousness and are based on targeted actions in the depth consciousness. So I can solve very concrete problems in a variety of ways, remove blockages and better achieve a higher level of consciousness with my concrete wishes. If you have learned self-hypnosis correctly, it is also easy to use and needs little time. You get a detailed guide.

Universal consciousness

The universal consciousness is independent of their material existence but associated with them. In the material existence, the key to creating the creative development of universal consciousness, through its body, it's thinking and feeling. Therefore, they are supported by him so that they can optimally advance this dynamic development. That's logic.

The following things should be considered:

1. Although material existence is needed for further development, it limits our consciousness and thinks on the other side. Since they are limited only to the material side of existence. To completely understand the material world, we would have to be outside of her and that would be absurd for development. As a result, there is no absolute knowledge, but always only a further development in our limited world.

2. Universal consciousness supports this process of development in the material world, with information and creation of correct cooperation offers, because, as explained, only by the material world can develop itself even further.

So there is a correlation. This relationship must be recognized correctly and used. We can build with our thinking and feeling this interaction. It works best about our depth awareness.

Finally, let's summarize how you can use the holistic news to get faster to your wish for fulfillment.

To better use this holistic, you need:

1. Strengthen your body and keep healthy.

2. Improve her thinking in which eliminates errors based on prejudice and beliefs.

3. Understand and accept the language of the feelings,

4. Dismantling blockages in their depth consciousness and learn how to use the source of communication with universal consciousness.

5. Body, thinking, feelings, depth awareness, and universal consciousness are connected directly to each other and form a whole. Think and feel like part of this whole.

6. Development of the creative force for the wishes

In the last twenty years, many investigations and experiments show how thoughts and feelings can change our material world and how information and cooperation on a higher level of consciousness, act on our material life. I already wrote about it. It is no longer a pure theory of faith and logic, but in reality, even if some are still doubting. In the course of my remarks, I will lead to underpinning further case studies.

It's about it now: How can you use these findings? What opportunities and methods are there to meet your wishes with the help of universal consciousness? So far, I have given you detailed information about which requirements you need to create and what you have previously prevented from it. I have demonstrated them methods of how they can clear these obstacles out of the way. You can now go to your desired filling.

6.1 Pull Balance

Proceed as follows:

Write down your current situation in keywords. Write only everything you have in positive. Only positives, leave everything negative way. Briefly describe everything positive in your actual situation. Feel joy and gratitude for what you already have. Formulate it too. Do not write about what you are dissatisfied with or what it's lacking. And certainly not, do nobody alleged for the negative aspects in their current life.

They get positive feelings. They need them to find their heart wishes and formulate properly.

Some examples:

1. I have a family I love. My husband and I have a job with which we can supply ourselves and our two children well. We love ourselves and the children feel salvaged with us. I have good friends with whom I can laugh and help me in need. I'm very grateful for all that.

Do not write here that you can no longer pay the rates of your loan or have too little time for your children. All this and much more you can easily wish and find solutions through hypnosis.

2. I am currently a Hartz IV receiver and get my rent for the apartment and have enough to live. Now I have

the time to look for something else in peace, better than ever before, and what makes me enjoy. The cards are remixed. No matter what situation I am also just, everything is possible if I want it.

Your whole disappointment and humiliation, which you may have already experienced as Hartz IV receiver, your entire bitterness, are understandable but let's getaway. That does not take you a little further. Wish and then simply plan your professional and private success in the next step.

3. I have a paid job. Have a nice apartment and a great car. I like to travel and was already on all continents of this earth. I can enjoy my life and am grateful for that.

Do not write that you are just before burnout because you make the job and that you feel alone because you leave the women or men again and again. All wishes to get happy then write up in the next step.

And so you can continue these examples, but I think the principle is understood. Write everything briefly that you already have and what you are satisfied and happy with and omit omission. Then formulate your heart wishes.

6.2 Set the right personal wishes

Everything in the universe is geared towards development and growth. So also the universal consciousness. So align your wishes afterward.

It does not bring anything if you want things that can only refer to your advantage and bring other disadvantages. Sometimes without it is aware. This creates no growth, but only in the best case a shift in your favor. Such wishes will not come true.

Here are some short rules for an explanation. In the section "Self-hypnosis exercises" I then go more detailed.

Rule one:

If you do not want a specific partner in which you are just in love or your (n) Ex. You do not know if that's good for the other or if you really can build a permanent happy relationship. Even if you are convinced right now. If you want a happy relationship instead. That's actually what you want. If it is the one you have chosen or your ex, then it will happen. But it can also be one or other (r), which you still get to know.

Rule two

Do not wish to talk before a job interview that you get this training or job. Maybe there is an equivalent or better application candidate for this training or this job that can contribute exactly as much or more to grow. This wish cannot come true. Just wish a training or a job that fulfills and continues. That can also be something concrete. Maybe then it works with this application interview and if not then something better for you. What your desire meets more and will continue in the long run. Do not doubt it.

Rule three

Do not want yourself in the dispute or competition that you win. That depends directly against others who then lose. Wish yourself in the dispute simply justice and in the competition the highest spiritual or physical energy that can grow over it.

The universal consciousness meets your wishes only if you are associated with cooperation and creating growth for anyone involved.

Do not wish a lottery win. For this, they do not need cooperation that could give you universal consciousness. Therefore, it does not contribute to growth. Also not for you.

If you wish for a happy relationship, then the right partner is also happy with you. Both grow.

Wish yourself prosperity and wealth and imagine how you float in luxury, then the desire will not come true. But if you want prosperity and wealth to use for your safety and the whole development, let it flow and bring other people to further development or help you to help people, then this wish is true. Feel how well with wealth and wealth feels. You can also wish for concrete things, such as a specific car or a house, etc. As a result, they flow money and also use other people with the use of these things as a rule. See it and feel it.

Some believe if you always give, then it will fall back at some point. Mostly that does not work. There is simply no cooperation if you do not send your wishes for your wishes and do not participate directly in the creation process. There is no development. The universal awareness does not value your actions and therefore does not reward them. Only when you send out your wishes, it is looking for cooperation that uses all. This gives you much more and contributes to the development.

Formulate your wishes clearly and unmistakable. So formulate what you want and not what you do not want.

Leave all formulations like, it would be nice if ... I do not want... I would be happy if... I would like to.... And so on. Tell me clearly what you want. If you want prosperity and wealth then they say that too and imagine the concrete picture. Feel it. Please do not forget to visualize it with the entire goal of further development (as described above). If you have the desire for a partner, then tell it clearly and clearly. Visualize this relationship without introducing a concrete partner to you. But see this partnership in front of your eyes and feel how happy you are there. I think the principle is understood. In the self-hypnosis exercise, there is more

Write your wishes. This is important. It is known that everything you write is also fertilized in your memory and thus can also get better in your depth consciousness. This allows you to read your wishes again and possibly improved in the formulation. If you have improved it, rewrite the final formulation again. Read your wishes more often and feel how good it feels when you are fulfilled. Are you grateful for that?

It can only be one wish or several. As a rule, not more than three or four, otherwise you may not be able to concentrate strong enough on each request in the requesting process. Formulate your wishes short and short, one to two not too long sentences without a comma.

We know that feelings are the universal language. Transport the feelings with your wishes together into universal consciousness. The more honest and stronger the feelings, the faster the wish goes true.

Rule one
Deposit all wishes with strong feelings. Emotions you have when the desire has come true.

Rule two
Only use positive feelings like love, joy, trust. Gratitude should be included in every request.

Rule three
Listen to your feelings. It often comes as an answer, as a reference for good cooperation at your request from universal consciousness. If you do not value feelings with your mind, then you often do not understand it and your wish remains unfulfilled.

Do not doubt, but feel gratitude because they are sure that they get what they want. If you feel a sincere gratitude, no room is for doubt.

Rule four
Trust in the holistic nature of your existence and the law that everything evolves. Even if there is something destroyed somewhat, because only because it can develop something new better. If you are aware of it, then you do not doubt that you will evolve and get support.

Rule five
Read and feel this sentence: "Who doubts, has already lost." Everyone can understand that. So if your wishes are to be true, then you do not doubt. It's your wishes that only know you. So it costs you absolutely nothing,

not even your image in the banners, if you are convinced inwardly firmly and not doubt.

How can I be sure that I have found the right wishes?

Sometimes it is not so easy to find his heart desires or to determine. Personal living conditions or dependencies of other people, as described in the book, often make it difficult for us. If you have formulated your heart wishes, but are not quite sure, then apply the already described mirror technology.

Imagine a mirror and look deep into the eyes, down to your soul. Think of a heart's desire. Which feelings will contact you if you imagine that this wish has just come true? Listen to your inner voice. At that moment your soul will give you the right answer. Hold this answer. Do not rate them. It feels great and is happy, then it's a real desire. But even under not exactly to define feelings come, it is not a matter of the heart. Even if you stick to it from otherwise, he will not come true.

Now make it with every wish and find your heart wishes.

Desire fillings from my life

Finally, some examples from my life, how to realize wishful performance. Of course, I have already had many wishes. Many of them did not come true.

Especially at the beginning I still had my difficulties, since I was not free of prejudice, false beliefs and had to let go of my problems. But that has now become much better.

Since this is my personal experience and I'm not an anonymous person, of course, I will not just describe the wishful fillings that are very personal. But even small wishes that everyone can have so shown how well wishful fulfillment works.

Example one: on home search

A few years ago, I came back to Berlin because of long-term freelance activity. The task was very interesting and after a conversation, I also got a good deal. The problem was only, I should start already in three days. Otherwise, they would have taken another applicant. Since I lived 210 kilometers from Berlin at this time, I need an apartment in Berlin. That's what I said to the boss, who led the conversation with me too. I asked him if he did not know where I get a room so fast. He answered me, "That's not my problem. I do not let myself clamp myself to solve your problems. They are successful coaches, now they show what they can. "

I had time until the next morning at 9:00 to tell the company my decision, whether I can start there in three days or not. I did not know anyone in Berlin, where I could have temporarily stayed. A pension was too expensive for me then, so I was looking for a room on the internet, which was very difficult in Berlin at that time. Many searched for months afterward. I wanted and needed this job. I started with the room search at noon. For me, beyond question, I had to find a room until the evening. My thoughts and wishes were aligned. I had agreed on two sightseeing dates in the evening. I got a room near my future facility. A furnished room in an old villa. This bordered with a miracle. It was not very nice and not for the duration. Since living is very important to me, I focused on my desire for a new apartment. Only a month later I found two streets, even in a villa, with very nice landlords a beautifully furnished two-room apartment, at a sensationally low price for Berlin.

But since I was a furnished apartment, this was not a final solution for me. I wanted an apartment with own furniture I had currently stored. Besides, I wanted to have room for a coaching room in my apartment to work there as a coach. That's why I was looking for it. But now I had more time. Who knows Berlin definitely knows how difficult, that is to find an apartment at a reasonably affordable price. But since I had time, I also searched them in a coveted residential area, regardless of the low chances of success. In fact, after a year, there was two sightseeing in one day. Both apartments did not correspond to my idea. After visiting them, I was walking aimlessly through this district and looked at the houses in which I would love to live. I came to a street that was right in a forest. Quiet and with beautiful houses. I felt enchanted. Directly at the forest in Berlin, something was my dream. That's how I felt it. Of course, it was a coveted road in an already coveted residential area. I wish you want to live here. But did not have a rental offer anywhere.

I visited two other apartments in the next three weeks but this road did not go out of my head and every time I thought about it came over me a great feeling, how nice it would be there. Three weeks later I found a housing offer. An apartment three-room apartment on this street. I was clear immediately. That's your apartment. I called the landlord. He had given a permanent sightseeing date. During this time, all interested parties were able to look at the apartment. That was so common in Berlin. I do not know why but I called him and told him that I'm not interested in such a mass tour. So asked him if he can make an individual viewing date with me. He gave me an appointment, one hour after the official sightseeing date. So if all interested parties had already seen the apartment and could decide. Of course, my chances were still lower. But I did not see that. I told him if it's my apartment, then I get it too. I came to this appointment and first asked if she's still to have. Then the landlord showed me a stack of applications, with salary records of applicants. But said he'll look at that in peace and then decide. It did not impress me or let me doubt, though I probably was not the best with my documents.

So I visited the apartment with him. She was ideal for me. Everything also voted the rental price, which lay under the average of such an apartment in this residential area. So I could afford an apartment of 86sqm here. That was almost incredible. In the sightseeing, we talked and told about our self-employed work. We got understood immediately. He also realized how excited I was from the apartment and finally asked me if I want them. I told him that would be my dream. Without seen my application documents at all, he handed me his hand and said, then hit them. The apartment is you. I had my dream apartment and thanked me at the universal consciousness.

Example Two: The car of my dreams

For my life, I like to drive fast cars. I always dreamed of a black sports car with red leather sitting. However, I could not even afford that at that time. That's how I drove my old VW Golf back then. But was not dissatisfied with it, on the contrary. At that time I work freelance as a psychological supervisor with social-deserved young people. It was a fixed daily working time. In my work, I was very successful and had a conversation with the director after a year. There he offered me firm work. Since he realized that I was not so enthusiastic about it, he moved to the offer, of course, I could also work freelance. The hourly rate has been increased.

Since my old Golf really was in the last trains and already rust had scheduled, I asked him for a service vehicle. No staff there had a service vehicle. I knew that, but you can try it. Unfortunately, he also rejected that with me but offered me an interest-free credit so that I can buy a new car. That's what I accepted. But did not want to do so much debt and was with 10000, - € to peace. A used car did it too. My wish for a sports car still had to wait. Nevertheless, I first looked after used sports cars. You never know. And actually, I found a BMW Z3, it was only 86000km dangerous and cost 8500, Euro. The average price for such a car was at that time at 14500, - Euro. The ad was online for an hour. That was incredible. I immediately shouted. It reported a woman. She told me, she hitherto worked in a car dealership at BMW and is now changing to Mercedes. Of course, it cannot drive there with a BMW to work there. She has chosen this reasonable price, which is a purchase price for car dealers because they want to make the sale quickly. The car is perfectly fine. She gives me a private one-year warranty. And it was exactly the car, which I always wanted, black with red leather sitting. I was overjoyed and buy it on the phone unseen. It was brought me and I never regretted it. Of course, I did not know anything about fulfillment and universal consciousness but was still very grateful for it.

Example Three: My Talisman
In my research, I also leave stories about experiments, as has been proven that objects have memories. I realized that churches, castles, castles, or very old houses had influenced me and my emotions. So that interested me. So I came to the theory like Talismans. Even if that was not scientifically detectable, I found it fascinating. Especially since faith alone can already have a positive effect.

That's why I was looking for a suitable Talisman for me. I met the very interesting story about the Atlantis ring. I knew immediately, that was my talisman. Now I was looking for where to buy such a ring. I found it on eBay. There some were offered, but only one corresponded to the original. The seller offered this ring three times. It was made of silver and the entry-level price was 10 euros. I offered one of the three rings, with the lowest term and said to him with a solid emotional conviction, if you belong to me, then you come to me too. I visualized my Atlantis ring, as I wore him by my hand and his energy in my body-wide. I saw them built a shield around me. After that, I was very busy for a few days and just briefly thought about it.

After four days I got a message from eBay, "Congratulations you bought the Atlantis ring". I looked straight on eBay and noticed that only the ring on which I had commanded was sold for 10 euros. The other two rings with a later expiration period of 30 to 50 minutes, from the same seller, with the same photo, had not expired yet and we're already at 28, - and 33, - Euro. It was totally unlikely that bidders may have offered and overboard for this ring for 20 or 25 euros for this ring, not on my ring, which runs as first if the current offer is only 10 euros. But if they had done it, the ring would not have come to me, because I had no time to offer. For which price the two other rings have been sold, I did not pursue anymore. It was not important to me. I told him: "O.K. You belong to me ", and could hardly wait until he arrived with me. After putting him in my hand, I pushed thanks to giving to the universal consciousness. I always carry my Atlantis ring day and night. He will be my companion in my whole remaining life.

I could tell many of these stories. Surely many also know examples from their own lives. It works. Learn to use consciously. Not all my wishes have been fulfilled so far, but I'm sure that will come. Everything is possible with the conscious creative wish to fulfill. The better one is in it, the more effective it works.

7. Self-hypnosis exercises

There are many ways to go to hypnosis. Mache uses objects such as a pendulum, rotating slices, or just the strong fixing to an object. Certainly, that's also away. In my opinion, it is also possible without such aids. I describe here a way to the hypnosis, as I have already applied you a hundredfold and how it works equally for self-hypnosis.

How fast you go into hypnosis, is very different. In one, it succeeds very fast and immediately at the first start. Others need a little more time. Especially in self-hypnosis, some exercise may be required. Although everyone can visualize, it falls hard to do that aware. This just requires a little practice. If you have become a professional, you often need only a few seconds and have to use this way I do not want to describe them now.

After all self-hypnosis exercises, I describe a short version. You can use them if you master the entry into the deep hypnosis and the language of the feelings. This allows you to put yourself in deep hypnosis and communicate with the universal awareness for seconds or minutes.

The place for the hypnosis

Looking for a place for self-hypnosis, where you feel comfortable. Many prefer a quiet room where they feel safe and feel safe. A room, maybe with objects that mean a lot. A room where you feel many positive energies. This room does not necessarily have to be dark. On the contrary, mostly it is more pleasant to be in a light-flooded room. Others prefer a room outdoors. Here you feel free and can best relax. Test it.

In my coaching room, I have given special importance to colors, pictures, and energy symbols. With a lot of light, wood, and pleasant odors.

The body position in hypnosis

Take a position in which you feel completely relaxed. Please pay attention to it. Which you have to keep this position for a long time without it then presses or becoming unpleasant. Many cross the arms behind his head or lay on the chest. This is usually unpleasant in deep relaxation. If you lie, put the arms best to the side. Also, ensure that you do not start freezing. Even if it does not appear necessary at the beginning, cover themselves. Some feel more relaxed in an armchair. Just test it for yourself. Later, they can easily perform the self-hypnosis in any position.

In my coaching room, I use an adjustable, very soft massage bench. Here I can set the lying position individually.

Further environmental factors in hypnosis

As a rule, it should be a quiet space. Avoid disturbing noises from the outside. With more and more exercise you will not bother noises and you can also relax deep if it's louder... Give your room good scents that you like. Often, with MP3 and CD, sounds are offered to support hypnosis. Test it in self-hypnosis. In the self-hypnosis, run conversations (we will come later) will usually be disturbing. In my hypnosis, I do not use that as the client should focus fully on my voice.

The right time of hypnosis

For self-hypnosis, I recommend choosing a time in which they are awake and rested. Usually, this is still washing in the morning and before breakfast. So they go relaxed and with new energy in the day. This morning's hypnosis does not have to take long. Maybe 15 to 20 minutes. Later, already 5 to 10 minutes are enough. If possible, carry it out every day. Take the five minutes for it. You will notice it is worth it. In Hypnosis, you quickly find the rituals that will help you to dive into your depth consciousness without further expenses.

Taking greater problems you need more time in the beginning. If you cannot apply the time in the morning, you have to look for another time. In this case, it is important to go to hypnosis without time pressure. But you should not be tired, otherwise, they will sleep.

When I notice in my coaching practice that a client is tired, I make a few energetic physical exercises with him before hypnosis to revive him. For example, I let them run them or him a few minutes of a loose hip-swiveling in the room. You can do that at home. This will increase your energy flow very quickly and are awake.

If you have prepared everything so far then you can start with relaxation:

Go into self-hypnosis

Put yourself relaxed and close your eyes. Position your arms to lose besides your body, breathe quietly and out. Make sure that you are getting heavier with every exhale and deeper. Say in thought "the deeper I sink all the more comfortable and more relaxed I feel"

You will feel it is always more relaxed.

Put yourself to a place that you know, where you are very happy and feel very comfortable and sure. It may also be a fantasy location. It has been shown that the unrealistic is the place where you feel comfortable, the deeper you go into hypnosis. There are no limits to their imagination. But it should only be such a place to come back to every other hypnosis.

Try this place to see in a dream in front of yourself. Take a look, the contours are getting more and more clear. You may hear birds and smell the flowers. Sometimes it helps if you look at a nice place in advance or smells of a flower or perfume. Relax, you are now in another, spirit world or if you want, in your dream world, and everything is possible there.

In the deep awareness

You will see a comfortable wide lounger in this place. They go to this lounger and lay on them. She is very soft and comfortable. They are now on this soft comfortable lounger in the middle of their favorite place. That feels wonderful. They feel free and safe.

With this lounger, you drive very slowly and quietly deeper. The deeper you sink, the free and safer you feel. Ever deeper. They pass an invisible gate. They feel a small but pleasant resistance and then they fall very deep again. That's pleasant. Now you are on a bright beautiful walk. It is the gait of their depth consciousness. They walk along the corridor and right are loud doors. They walk past doors. The further you go, the better they feel. Now stay at a door. They turn to this door and see a sign. On this sign stands "room of feelings". You read it again "room of feelings."

They open this door and stand on a summer meadow, see the green grass and the colorful flowers. Red poppies, blue bluebells, yellow butter flowers. You see how colorful butterflies flutter over the meadow. They stand in the middle of the meadow and breathe fresh oxygen-rich air. They feel infinitely free and happy.

Now, look around. They look over the meadow and see in the middle of their big single tree. It is your life tree with a thick trunk and a green leaves crown. They go to this tree and hug the big trunk. They push their whole body firmly to the trunk and feel a light vibrate. They feel their life energy. This energy now flows into your body. They feel pleasant warmth spreads into their whole body. They feel a pleasant light tingling in their whole body. They feel the energy that strengthens their body. That feels good. They feel strong and free now. Now they release themselves from their tree and have arrived in deep awareness.

For example, you can do releasing how previously described. Let persons, false beliefs, prejudices, and much more.

If you have enough exercise, you can shorten this way and go straight to the meadow to your life's tree. If you try it and notice that it does not work so really, then extend the way again. Do not put pressure under pressure. It's just a matter of time without compulsion. But always start on the meadow and embrace your life tree. Feel the energy and download it. This is the prerequisite for success in all further steps.

From this location, you can now send your heart wishes to your depth awareness and quickly and unadulterated the universal consciousness.

There is a second option that is especially helpful for some. I would like to introduce them to them. Just try out what's best for you.

Here is another expanding option:

After taking energy in your life tree and have arrived in your depth awareness, meet a companion on the meadow. An angel or a person they have come up with a person from the past, which is very important to them, a person whose body has already died and who they know or worship them. That can also be a great personality out of history. No matter, it is a companion from the universal consciousness.

So a direct contact. This accompanying you on your journey through your depth awareness and your wishes. It may only look at the friendly and confident, show them pictures or they can talk to him. Try it.

Let's get to the individual wishes.

7.1 Love and luck

The desire for love and a happy partnership is probably the most intimate and most desire of people. This wish is directly linked to the cooperation of another person. Therefore, stay with your desire as neutral as possible to find the right partner with which you will be permanently happy and with you. This applies to single. For people in a relationship, it is about possible problem solutions in the partnership.

For single

So your wish could be: I want a partner with which I am happy and he with me. I want to give him my love, my trust, just as he wants to give me.

To formulate it unambiguously. What do you wish? What would you like to give your partner and what would you like to have from it so you will be happy in this regard? Of course, you can change the wording according to your wishes. But do not refer to this wish to a specific person. This could not come true. I already explained the reasons. But you will get a happy lasting love relationship with this desire. If it's the partner you may have in mind, then it will happen anyway. If not comes a better one. You can be sure.

Here is the further way in your depth awareness:

If you have experienced disappointments in love relationships with which you have not finished properly, then do the following:

"You see, have just hugged your life tree, there's a light beam on the meadow. So big that you can put it in there. They go there and put themselves with the back. Now you feel like your body is getting lighter and starts to float up. You now hover up in the light beam. You see down and notice how a shadow has been released from her body. He dissolves out of her back and floats down. Now feel that you feel lighter and free. It dissolves a shadow from your body and one more. Every time a shadow triggers your body, make you feel easier and free. They feel quite freed. Now come up at the top. "

For single, which have already completed with their former love relationships, it is sufficient if you go from your life tree only through a light gate.

"There they are back on a meadow. This time she is still brighter and colorful. There you can see a person. You feel immediately, it's your life partner. Full of expectation and joy they go to him. You see his beautiful bright eyes and feel he brings you strong feelings. Then they are very close to them and cannot help themselves otherwise. You feel his body. It is wonderful. Your bodies merge into each other and their feelings overwhelm them. You now know exactly, you have found the right partner. They dissolve from each other and feel trust and certainty. That's the person in your life. They kiss you. They feel very intense the kiss. It crawls in your whole body. Then they say goodbye. They are very happy about it because they know that they see him again soon and then stay together. "

Avoid staying here forever here, even if it's your heart's desire. If it leads to the growth of both permanently, then it will come like that. But it can change something with one or both in the course of life and grow only by changing. Set up your wish only and alone on growth, otherwise, your request will not come true.

"They go back to the light, through the light. You are back on your life tree. They feel very happy. You know you will encounter these people and they are looking forward to it. Then put themselves in the grass under their lives and feel great gratitude. They close their eyes and count slowly to three. At three, they open their eyes and awakens again from hypnosis. The happy feeling and the certainty they have taken them up. "

SHORT VERSION

Go into deep hypnosis and meet your partner. Hug him and feel the strong love and attachment to each other. They are sure they will meet.

For people in a relationship
People in a happy relationship have already fulfilled this heart's request. It looks different if you have problems in a relationship and want to change that. In this case, you must talk to your partner before. If your partner wants to improve your relationship again. If it is also a matter of the heart of him or he generally doubts about this connection or if he may be completed inside. Only if it is a matter of the heart of your partner, then your desire for a happy relationship with him has success. If not, then leave it. It's lost time and energy, so hard that sounds.

If your partner wants hearts, like you, that your relationship will get better again, then you can go to hypnosis as with single.

Only this time you encounter your partner. Hug him and kiss him, with the feeling like it was the first time. They go hand in hand over the meadow, listen to music, and dancing in the meadow. Then you cordially laugh and hug yourself again. They say goodbye with the certainty that everything will be good and beautiful again.

7.2 Health

Not only people with health problems with health and long life. Of course, some people reveal vehemently a long life because they see themselves as falling people. But that too is just a prejudice. Being healthy, people can also go to old age. The picture of the old attractive person is about to change. Slowly but incessant. I am convinced that generations already live today, a different picture preserved.

Of course, it will be up to you whether you take off this prejudice. But then you do not want it either. That would be a shame. The older man becomes spiritual and physical health and fitness, the more he can contribute to development through his greater experiences and deeds. According to today's findings of biologists, man can be in health and fitness 130 years old and genetic engineering is already out of very different lifetimes. Why should you degrade yourself with such a prejudice itself and put yourself against further development?

For a healthy and long life

"After hugging your life tree, put yourself under his crown into the grass. Now you feel, as heat in your body is moving out of the ground. It is the energy of your life tree. This warmth now feels you throughout the body. Like a wave, this energy goes through its body from top to bottom and from bottom to top. Feel this wave as it flows through your body. She also captures the last cell of her body. This wave full of life energy cleans and repaired all its body, up to the single cell. They see how sick cells will be healthy again, how weakly luminous cells start back to brighten. They see this wave as they slowly push all the dirt they rinsed out of their cells. You see the wave with all the dirt. It looks like dust.

Now, this wave comes to your stomach. There she changes her flow direction and circles with all the dust around her stomach. Like a slower strudel, the whole dust turns in a circle. This circle we very warm. Always warmer. That's pleasant. You see how the dust transforms through the heat into smoke and slowly flows from your belly button. The whole smoke flows out of her navel button. You see how the smoke flows out of them and they feel better and better. The feeling of happiness is getting stronger, the more smoke flows out. Now the power stops. The whole smoke, the whole dirt is out of them. They feel how the wave can flow again life energy through their body. You see the wave and everything are clean and sparkles. They feel their body, how strong he is. Now they are back.

If you have a helper, then you can do the following:

They meet their angel on the meadow, the direct representative of universal consciousness. Without talking, your angel knows what you want. They want their body to be healthy and strong. Her angel transforms into an energy body and enters them from behind. He is now in your body. They feel him in themselves. They feel his energy. It feels very good and familiar. You now feel like this energy into the single-cell penetrates your body, repaired and strengthening it. That makes you feel. It starts upwards from the feet. It's warm and pleasant. Where you have problems it will be very warm and you stay a time at this point, then go on. Sometimes it will also be warm, in places where you do not feel any problems. But they allow repair and enjoy this wonderful intimate association with their angel. They feel this healing energy. Her angel occurs from her body and transforms and gets his figure again. They are full of happiness and love. They embrace him and him. They thank him for this wonderful healing.

Now they go full of happiness and energy over the meadow and come on away. He has a name tag. This is life. It is the way of your years.

They are now alone or with their angel on this way. In the beginning, there is a sign with its current age. It's a nice way. They go full of energy and joy along the way. At the edge of the way, they meet people who are friendly to them. Then come to a shield where you are ten years older. They keep walking. And ten years older and again. They feel, full of energy and joie de vivre. Again, they encounter people who are friendly to them.

They come to a lake. Meanwhile, they are around 80 years old. They go to the lake and pull out completely naked. They feel free and happy. Now you swim in the lake. They make strong trains and get ahead easily. With every swimming movement that brings you forward, you feel the pleasantly warm water as it flows past your body. This electricity takes you all your negative energy. It is pulled out of the water out them. It's a great feeling. They rise from the water again and feel the pleasant warm air as they dried their body. It is a strong attitude to life which spreads into your whole body. They feel alive and full of energy.

Now pull on and go on the way. You will not get tired and feel good. And again a sign, ten years later. It is wonderful this life. You see how the path goes on. He does not end. Whole, very back you see a bright light in which the path goes in. But they are going back to their meadow, to their life tree. Once there, they embrace their tree again full of joy and say goodbye to him today. They put in the grass and count to three. We woke up make you feel great and are full of joie de vivre. You feel that your body is healthy and fit.

Brief

They go straight to their tree. They embrace and welcome him. Place the meadow and leave the energy wave as described. Finally, see the smoke from your body. Feel strong and healthy afterward. Feel gratitude.

Or

Meet your angel from universal consciousness. He enters her body and they feel him in themselves. Then as described above. The angel comes out of them again. They feel healthy and strong. Full of life energy. That makes you happy. They embrace their angel and say goodbye to him.

Your life will then go as needed.

I am sometimes asked in my coaching: Can I wish for another loved one that he will be healthy again?

Of course, you can. Especially when it is an accident, where the person concerned is no longer able to wish for himself. Here, it depends on how strong your souls are connected in this life. The universal consciousness recognizes such connections. Only a few strong-minded people can also create such connections if they have not yet known these people. But that too is possible. So do not wish to heal but not with the thoughts and feelings like Do not leave me alone. What should I do without you and so on? But do you want yourself unselfish for your worked soul with which you feel closely connected, recovery? Then you can see a long happy life in the mind or hypnosis. Be grateful for this.

7.3 Success

Most people want to succeed in their lives. Success in the profession, success in school or studies, success in sport, and much more. People want to prove themselves and recognition, preserved in their social environment. Again, the success in the context of the further development of the whole can be seen and involved. Success should not be achieved at the expense of others. That would be a shift and no further development at best.

For example, such a wish could be as follows:

1. An actor wishes to succeed, and sees success on posters or sees enthusiastic people applauding him

2. An architect sees how his order books are filled and he works on a large project.

3. A power sportsman sees himself as he grows beyond himself and breaks the world record - do not see in the case as they stand on the winding staircase in the first place, so they affect the other athletes, which then not on the first Square should be.

4.   A pupil or student sees himself with an excellent degree as he leaves school and has a good job in his pocket.

5.   An unemployed or someone with a job he is very dissatisfied looks how he gets a new job that is much better than what he did before professionally.

You can continue this. But I think the principle is understandable.

Success to wish you can only refer to yourself, so your heart wishes, even if it is the success of a group in which you are a member. As already explained, you cannot wish for others. Of course, you can wish the whole group success, but your heart's desire, who should be sent out and true, can only refer to you. Obtain your heart's desire always what you want to achieve with it.

For example:

1. I want to grow beyond myself and can give everything to team players so that my team is successful.

2. In my team, I would like to fulfill my tasks with the best results and thus motivate the other members even more so that we achieve our goal together.

3. As a team leader, I always want to make the right decisions and support my members optimally at all, so that we are successful.

That too can be continued as desired. Think and just feel what you can do in the team or a group to be successful and wish you that.

Your wish for success

Depending on how your success wishes look, you can of course send it to the universal consciousness with your thoughts and feelings. In my work, especially two methods have been proven.

First method:

"They are in their depth awareness on their life tree. Now you see a door in his thick trunk. You open the door with a button that you press. The door opens and it is an elevator, bright and big. You go in this elevator and press the button down. The door closes and you drive down, you feel how the elevator moves down. Now you see a scale of one to five. One light, then two, then three, four, and then five.

The elevator stops and the door opens. They come out and stand in the light room. In the middle of the room, there are three large mirrors. They go to the first mirror that is far left. There they see scenes from their past, how and what they work. It's fun. They look at the scene and feel gratitude. They move away from this mirror and he expires. Then look in the mirror, which is in the middle of the room. Now they see scenes from their current work or activity. Again they feel gratitude. They move away from this mirror and he expires. Now look in the right mirror. There they see the future. Just as you wish. Now you see the scene of your success. For example, full date books, documents on the wall, etc. They feel great and happy. They feel how good it feels if they succeed.

Then move away from this mirror but he does not go out. You see how the other two mirrors slowly dissolve and the last mirror is in the middle of the room and brightly reflects your success scenes. They go to the elevator, turn up again and see how the mirror in the middle of the room, brightly illuminates the scenes of their success. Now you feel a depth of certainty that this success is true. They go to the elevator and drive up again. They feel like great it is. They are grateful. Arrived at her tree of life, put in the grass, as always counting to three and awakening. The feeling of success they took them up. "

This method is very effective for people who have learned to visualize well. Here you not only see things that you experience yourself, but also pictures in the mirror. That's not always easy at the beginning for some. If you succeed, then use this method. If you have a companion he can help you.

SHORT VERSION

They stand in a room with three mirrors. After that, how had you left the room again?

Second method

"They stand back after the greeting on their life tree and go to the meadow. There they come on away. This path has a name: away from success.

This path goes slightly uphill and leads to a mountain. It is a wonderful hiking trail. Right and left are forest meadows and occasional trees. They go cheerfully and full of energy slowly up. They feel inner peace. Nobody holds her. Sometimes they stop and enjoy the beautiful nature. Halfway they meet a small group of people. They are a bit off the way and nod very friendly. As if they know them. There is a familiar feeling. They nod and go on.

You now have an even better feeling. Certainty senses that everything you want to come true. They continue to go up the mountain full of joy and energy.

Almost arrived come across a mountain hut. They go to this mountain hut. At the door is a sign. This is the house of your success - full tension opens the door and goes inside. You are in a living room and although they have never been there, he gets involved. They feel very comfortable here. There is a diary on the table. This is your name. You open the calendar and see it is full. Fully with appointments for your business or service or on the wall, documents that document your success, or there are trophies on the windowsill, and so on. In this room, you will find everything that shows you your success. Are you happy? You made it. Full of joy, they emerge thanks.

They leave the house again. If you have already run so far then you also want to summit the mountain. It is not far anymore. On the way, you enjoy your success. They feel great. Arrived at the summit Look to the horizon on a wide beautiful landscape. They feel how big and beautiful this world is. They spread their arms and feel strong. Everything is possible. Everything could be achieved if you want it. If you work in a team, the other team members will meet at the summit. They welcome joyfully and enjoy their common success. Once again, thank you together. Then they go back with the happiness of success in their way, to their life tree. They focus on the meadow, count to three and awaken with the firm conviction that the desired success will arrive. "

SHORT VERSIO

NThey go into the house of their success. Then as described. Until they stand on the mountain and spread the arms far. They belong to them the world.
In my coaching, I am sometimes asked, especially for athletes, why they do not want to be on the winning podium. After all, it's the heart's desire for an athlete. Well, many or more than one, you want you to win. With this wish, they displace others who also have this wish. Only the best can win. So you prefer to be sure that you fully exploit your performance and grow beyond yourself so that you are the best or become.

They see themselves in the mirror as you play football plays, like a young god or handball, volleyball, etc. in an individual competition they jump further than before or are faster, higher, further than they were ever. That's the reason why you can be seen or satisfied with your services and can grow. You can also set ourselves very concrete targets in your desired fulfillment, such as what minimum size, how fast, etc. do not set a maximum size, because it will limit themselves. The chance to become a winner with this desire is much greater than to wish the victory.

The universal consciousness does not care who wins in a competition. But a winner does not necessarily have to contribute more to growth than another one who has given everything. Many competitive athletes know the feeling.

7.4 Prosperity

In my coaching, I often experience that clients are ashamed of desirable. In the section beliefs in the example of C. of a now successful entrepreneur, I have already entered.

Understanding prosperity, as a worry-free financial life, contributes to the development of all when:

1. Prosperity through high achievements that contribute to the development and do not arise at the expense of others.

2. Prosperity focuses on the safety and freedom of man and does not invest in decadent burden addiction.

3. Prosperity leads through the right security, better in the general public. There have always been wealthy people who have always done a lot for the general public and thus for the growth of all.

So wealth must always serve the development of all or the whole directly or indirectly. Such wishes of prosperity are fulfilled in the creative wish fulfillment, as long as it is a matter of the heart. So you want prosperity in this sense and you will be able to make a big contribution to the growth of the universe.

Prosperity in this sense is therefore built on performance. It is a prejudice, if not even with many a belief that people have different conditions and thus some more benefits can provide than others. This is wrong because it always refers to a subjective evaluation of performance. At least in people who were born healthy. Why:

1. Today we define services almost exclusively in the sense of our service company. Namely services and production of products that can be sold on the market. Even art or science is finally oriented to market economic conditions. So many benefits that do not prevail there.

2. Everyone thinks can be creative and born with special talents. Whether it's high intelligence, a particular talent, a high sensitivity, a special gift for intuition, and much others. Everything is equally important in universal awareness and can contribute to growth, even if it is not recognized in a market economy. In principle, everyone has to provide the prerequisites for growth. That finds recognition. Everyone can be wealthy.

3. The performance of which every person is born can be promoted or inhibited by external conditions, for example in the parents' home, orphanage, or school. But already in the preliminary phase. Become promoted then that usually takes place and to prosperity. Wealthy people should therefore promote the others and do not give mainly alms.

4. The promotion of others contributes to development, alms to a standstill. But that is not to be confused with the selfless support of people who are in an emergency. But people who give us permanently alms, so they can survive without promoting them, we automatically put on a siding on which they do not belong. Sometimes it is convenient on both sides.

5. The talents and talents of each person remain maintaining, even if they were inhibited so far according to previously deprived conditions. Thinking remains and thus the possibility of changing, in the sense, its talents and opportunities to develop and implement. To change his prejudices and beliefs and to use the creative wish fulfillment. Finally, to become wealthy. And not exclusively in the material sense.

This enumeration does not spring from my theoretical thinking, but from my practical experience. As a coach, I worked with entrepreneurs, artists, athletes, inventors, politicians, unemployed, socially disadvantaged adolescents, with so-called ADHD, and many others. All people have unique talents and investments that can be valuable and can contribute to the development of all.

No matter what situation you are in. You can think and have feelings! This creates her life creatively. Sometimes you need help. But if you are looking for help and desire to be honest in the creative wish fulfillment, then you will also get the right help. Sometimes they also notice it later, as they have experienced help. Everyone can reach everything. Practical examples from every situation I know enough. In this book, you will find everything you need to become happy, successful, and wealthy.

What do you see if you want prosperity? A house, a car, a great housing facility, a large bank account. Imagine the things that will mean prosperity for you according to your ideas. What creates your safety and freedom? What do you need? Imagine what you do with this prosperity. How well you feel for example if you drive in your dream car. How well they feel if they have friends, relatives, or strangers through their prosperity in a variety of ways to support their way. So how they live in prosperity and like this prosperity, directly and indirectly, radiates the development of others. Build all these ideas into self-hypnosis. I can now show you an example of this. In terms of content, you can then modify it to your wishes.

Example of a self-hypnosis: your desire for prosperity

"You are back on your life tree. After the usual welcome, they go slowly and leftover the meadow. There they meet their angel and they welcome themselves with joy. Her angel takes her to her hand and she goes on together. Your companion comes directly from the universal consciousness that meets the desire for prosperity as you imagine. He leads you to a very nice place on the edge of the meadow. In the forest at a lake. There is a beautiful house.

It is your house or a house with your apartment in it. Just as you have always imagined. You will see it in all details, with a large terrace, a beautiful garden, etc. You go in and feel at home. It is as a living in this house. They go through the rooms and everything is as it should be. They feel great and happy. They made it and are free of all money worries. There are bank statements on the desk of your study. You see how much fortune you own. At the same time, they think about what they do with this fortune. You see on the desk project documents. Brochures with projects they have already implemented and designs, about projects they want to do, etc.

They are proud of their achievements and their possibilities. These include social projects that are particularly important to them. You are grateful for you to have the opportunity to build or promote these projects. They feel great gratitude. Then leave your house again and meet your angel in front of the house, which smiles radiantly. You cannot help it. They go to him and hug him with gratitude and joy. They have hugged the universal consciousness and were also received by him full of love. There is no doubt that your wishes were accepted and come true. Then go back to your life's tree.

If you want to hug him because they are still full of joy and gratitude. They then set in the way and count to three and awaken full of joy, gratitude, and certainty.

Abstract: Your angel shows you your prosperity. Then as described. Until the grateful hug with him when they come back.

8. Power of self-hypnosis

In most cases, they have more than a heart's desire. Therefore, you do not need to go into several self-hypnosis. In the Power Self-hypnosis, I show you how you can transport that in hypnosis into universal awareness to your desired fulfillment.

This self-hypnosis application is based on long experience in the self-test and working with many clients in my coaching. It contains all visual and emotional aspects to perform optimally wishes. I'll explain it step by step.

Before we go to hypnosis, here are some tips:

1. Look at a part of a whole. All parts of the whole, as explained, are parts of them. Think and feel it. They cooperate and can fulfill their wishes. It consists of the body, thinking, feelings, depth awareness, and universal consciousness. With this conviction, it is easier and more effective in hypnosis.

2. If you can visualize well, then you are already at the advantage. Everyone has the prerequisite to visualize. But some falls hard in the beginning. Practice it by looking at something, then close the eyes and imagine this image. Or look at an item, cover it or go in a different room and then paint this item on a piece of paper. So train your visual imagination.

3. It is difficult for you to go to relaxation, then first check that you have created the right outer prerequisites as described in the book. Is there something you may be disturbed in the room or your current thought? Eliminate everything disturbing. Let time in the relaxation and do not put yourself under pressure. You can be sure, even if it takes longer in the beginning, over time it gets better.

Implementation of power self-hypnosis

Go as usual in relaxation and then in your depth awareness.

In the beginning, it is helpful to use the three stages described for this. So relaxed in and exhales that lead you deeper into relaxation. Click down the stairs, to your favorite place where you start visualizing and feeling. The lounger that she brings her to her deep awareness like an elevator. Finally, the embrace of your life tree, which connects you emotionally with the deep awareness.

"You stand on your life tree on the meadow and see your angel. They feel great pleasure. Go to your angel and hug him happily at the welcome"

The angel is the symbol of universal consciousness and so she should feel it. You have taken direct contact with you. With everything that happens now, they are accompanied and strengthened by the universal consciousness.

"Your angel enters her body from behind and fulfills it with warmth and energy. He is now in your body. They feel him in themselves. They feel his energy. It feels very good and familiar. They feel like this energy strengthens each cell into their body. They feel it, starting from the feet and further upwards. It's warm and pleasant. If you have health problems, it will be very warm at this point. This heat lingers a short time at this point until they feel really good. Then it goes on in your body. Sometimes it will also be warmer, where you do not feel a problem yet. But they leave it and enjoy this wonderful intimate association with your angel. You feel this wonderful healing energy. Her angel occurs again, this time from the front of them. They are full of happiness and love. They embrace him and him. They thank him for this wonderful strengthening of their body and their feelings.

It is a targeted activation of your body through the universal consciousness, about the language of feelings. Her body, like everything else, is crossed by universal consciousness. With this experience, you activate your universal consciousness very specifically to strengthen or heal your body. Leave your angel always from behind and leaving it from the front. It has been shown that so the process in the body and the subsequent result can be better explained and felt.

You can also carry out this process of strengthening or healing separately. If you have learned to quickly go into your depth consciousness, you can only apply it for one or two minutes at any time. It works better than any energy drink or such a medicine. But never forget the gratitude. As a result, they feel deep with the universal consciousness and it does not miss his effect.

"Now go hand in hand with your angel by the way to a light beam that meets perpendicular from the top of the meadow. He is big, so you can put in. Your angel asks you to put into what you do too. They are completely wrapped by the light and feel safe. Now you notice how you start floating in the light beam slowly up. They look down and see how the meadow slowly removed from them. They feel completely safe and safe in this beam.

Now you see shadow down to sink on the meadow. There they dissolve. Now you notice that these shadows come out of your back. They watch now as they released their backs. Every time a shadow triggers out of your back, feel a slight tingling and then feel good. Always better and easier, with every shadow that solves. Until all of them have come out and floated down where they dissolve. Now look up again and see a big light at the end of the beam. They are getting closer and the light is getting bigger. The closer you come, the happier you feel. She wants to go to this light. "

Everyone has unprocessed inhibiting experiences that are aware of him or has quickly associated in his depth consciousness to remember. No matter, all these experiences build more or fewer blockages. These blockages must be solved to optimally enter the creative wish-filling process. Light is positive energy. In it, they now lose these conscious and unconscious blockages in the form of shadows. It is necessary that you not only see these shadows but feel that they are always better. It is the way to liberate her blockages that can lead to fears, prejudices, or false beliefs and adversely affects their desired fulfillment, if not prevented. It will be easier for you to let go of everything in a short time. So take this path seriously.

"They come into the light and realize how their body converts itself into light and energy. Your twill consists of light and energy. They feel completely free. There in the light, you will see your angel again, which is also an energy body. They go to him. He takes her to her hand and takes you through a door to a large balcony. You see the whole universe. The stars and light mist, planets, and much more. It is an overwhelming sight.

They feel completely free. They are now with their angel as alighting on the large balcony of the universe.

Her angel takes her to her hand and leads her to the edge of the balcony. They look up the universe and see a very bright light in the middle, which approaches them. This light comes to them and completely envelops them. Now you have direct contact. "

After you have cleaned your body in the light beam completely, you can dissolve your physicality and become pure light and energy. They feel free. This leaves the material world for some time and can now immersion in the universal consciousness.

"Suddenly they are, physically, in a beautiful street. A road you know or who always imagined. A street in which you want to live. They come to a house and go inside. Now you are in your apartment. She is exactly the one you always wanted. But now it's your apartment. They feel overjoyed. They walk through the apartment and look at everything. Everything is really good. They feel they made it.

You know that you are in universal consciousness. Here your wishes come true and you know that it will now be a reality. They are happy and thankful for that.

You can see pictures on the wall. Then you are with your dream car. In another picture, you will see yourself in Africa in a school with loud children, which support you financially. They have enough money and can support them. They are grateful for that. They go farther through the apartment on the terrace. "

In this case, it's a nice apartment a car, and a social project in Africa. See all the things you want personally in your prosperity. Wish yourself prosperity through success and for the development of all. This can also be a company with satisfied employees. Who are happy to come to your work?

"On the terrace, they meet a man. He looks deep in the eyes and they know immediately. That's him. That's the partner with which you are happy and he with you. He is very familiar with them. They go to him and hug him. What a wonderful feeling! It's like merging. Then you kiss yourself and you are happy. He looks deep in the eyes, so they can look deep into his soul. They tend to be in love and trust there. Then he says to them, I am here for you. Afterward, they are back on the balcony of the universe and see how this bright beam moves back to the middle of the universe. "

In the encounter with your partner, focus on his / her body and eyes. Do not imagine a partner you know. Find all the qualities you want from him in the partner's soul. Above all, you feel. You have your heart wishes you now, directly in the universal consciousness. It is the strongest way to communicate and be true. Your wishes will be true.

"Now they are back with their angel as alighting on the balcony of the universe. They are still quite dazed by this happiness. They embrace their angel before gratitude because he guided them here. Now go back in the light room to the light beam that leads down.

They go into the beam of light and slowly sink towards the meadow. The deeper you sink, the more they take their physicality again. They feel their body again and that feels great. They are now back on the meadow. Your body feels strongly top. You enjoy this body with every step you go. Her angel sees them as friendly, smiles. Now they say goodbye to him, embrace him again, and thank him. They focus on the meadow and count until 3. They awaken with the feeling of everything will be true. "

This power hypnosis is the most effective I have developed in my many years of practice.

9. An extremely effective prayer for all

On the constant search and improvement of my creative wish finishing methods, I also dealt with the power of prayers years ago. There are many reports about the positive effects of prayers. Some reports call prayers superstitions. If you deal more intensively, then you come to the following results.

Prayers, where someone asks for himself, can rather come true, especially when he talks confidently with all his feelings. Also prayers for a person with which one is very associated mentally and he cannot pray for himself by illnesses, often have a positive effect. On this topic, I have already written in the request for the "Health" section.

Prayers are usually directed to God. Depending on the religion, the performance is different. However, what has the path to the creative desire fulfillment with a prayer to God, is the wishes about feelings, beliefs, and gratitude directed to the universal consciousness.

I had now considered when I disperse the prayer on "Father ours you are in heaven", so no one appeal, which stands somewhere outside about me, but the universal consciousness appeal, which is a part of me, then the prayer gets one completely different direction. One direction where wishes to be accepted where they can be fulfilled.

So with this goal, I developed a prayer for myself, which I spoke daily in the morning. Over time, I recommended it to good clients from me and then have it in my e-book "coaching too: the seven mental laws of success. After Chopra, published. The result was, there was a great positive response. With such a big consent, I did not expect him. Even Christians pray the "father our" and then my prayer. That's why I would like to imagine it in this book, explain it, and for the first time give instructions on how to apply it more effectively.

It is certainly not a new religion, but to better use our potential of our existence of our potential.

Close the eyes.

The prayer

"Father you are the consciousness of this world"

Although the word father is very reminiscent of the father, so this word is emotionally bound to be something we come from and that is part of us. Of course, you can also say something differently. I did not find anything more appropriate. Maybe you should rather use a well-known term and when to seek a different other than the second choice.

You must have a firm convinced feeling in this sentence: It gives you, universal awareness (father), you are part of me and I'm talking to you, in the universal language of feelings.

"Fulfill me with your mind, your love, and your energy. Let me be part of your strength. "

The spirit of universal consciousness has the task of every human being for his development to give everything he wishes to contribute to development as a whole. If you tell the spirit, then feel the mind in your head.

Love is the strongest positive feeling of existence. Therefore, connect with this feeling in this prayer. Feel the love in your heart when speaking this word, so strong you can.

Energy is the force that brings us forward in our material existence. Feel this energy and this power in your whole body at the moment you speak. So make a break after each word, so you can feel it too.

"Protect the shadows of the past, the present, and the future. Because I am only a human, vulnerable, and missing on earth. "

We have already talked about these shadows in this book in detail. Some blockades develop through our actions, such as fears, love cumbers, grief, doubts, etc., prejudices and false beliefs and lead us in false cooperation.

"Leave your mind, your love, and your energy through me as part of you, on the earth."

Here they feel that they want to use these forces of universal consciousness, which are always already in them and they want to use through streams, to contribute as part of the whole to develop. Feel how good it feels to be a creator. Feel love and gratitude that you can be.

"And give me love and happiness in a partnership, health, and a long life, success, and prosperity, so that I can use all my forces."

Here you can use your heart desires. Visualize each of your heart desires, as in the hypnosis, and feel how good it feels if it is reality. So let's time with your kind wishes in this prayer. After each heart's desire, take a break and visualize it. Feel how good it is that you can better use all your strength for the whole. They do not feel like a single person, but are much more, namely a part of the entire creation.

"I thank you, father."

Feel deep gratitude for this moment and send them off because they will give them all in this material life, which makes you experience luck and fulfillment.

If you want, try it with this prayer. Correctly, it contains everything for your desired filling. The best times are to go in the morning or the evening before sleeping or in bed before falling asleep.

10. Live holistically with your wish-fulfilling

If you have done everything right, your wishes still do not meet alone. You get direct and indirect cooperation offers you need to recognize and then act. These offers that give them universal consciousness, however, are often not easy to recognize with our mind.

They inevitably start thinking. What do I have to do so my wishes come true? Which cooperation do I need? And so on. They focus in their actions on the practical implementation of their wish for their previous experiences and knowledge.

With that, they set themselves up and cut a lot too much. As a result, they do not recognize the actual possibilities, including cooperation opportunities that they manifested because of their wishes they manifested. Therefore, in many seminars and books on this topic is often said: "After which you have set your wishes, go." That's true, according to my experiences only pleased, is even wrong in some way.

Her consciousness, thinking, and feeling are firmly anchored in the material world. That's right because your job is to develop new feelings and new thoughts where you are working in the material world. Thus, they develop, as explained, and also the whole.

Although they have learned how they give creative desires into the universal consciousness they also have to learn how to recognize and implement this help they receive. They must be once more aware that universal awareness is also a part of them, with whom they can communicate about feelings at any time. After that, you have to align your thinking and acting. So you have to stay a part of the whole constantly. So you recognize the possibilities that it offers you.

Therefore, do not only use your mind and its ego. But connect with the whole to make your wishes come true.

How can you build constant contact with universal awareness and heart desires?

Create walkers in your habitats, where you always feel, how well it feels when your wish has come true.

As a result, it does not doubt them themselves and focuses unequivocally on their heart wishes, which are always present. Since they are constantly talking about their feelings, learn, over time to recognize feelings and intuitions that lead to their desire for fulfillment. So they use not only their minds but open their emotional intelligence, with the aim of their wish fulfilled. So they also recognize the many possibilities offered.

You have to create these forces yourself. For example, I have made my Atlantis Ring, from which I've reported, only for strong power, where I attributed it to him full of conviction and feelings, that he gives me protection and happiness. So I got him and always feel that he does. One says: "Faith (certainty) puts mountains" and that's the same way because we are releasing information here and help.

Important: Do not wish your wishes to come true. But just feel how good it feels when she had become.

It is helpful to seek objects that are already sought by predominantly a positive effect. It is much easier to manifest your feelings. In principle, however, it is completely for the desired filling, no matter which items you choose. It is important only that these objects are always present in their lives. You should be able to wear or watch more often. Again and again, remember how well it feels when your wishes are fulfilled. Then they transport these feelings and information more and more in their depth awareness and sets themselves there over time. So it seems even if you do not think about it or see your power place or see. They have built a bridge for universal consciousness in this way without having to constantly think about it. This will help you better the right collaborations without it being aware of it.

In my coaching, therefore, I often set the wishes during the deep hypnosis into an object. This will be stronger right from the start. This helps in the desire for fulfillment but also in eliminating fears, self-confidence weaknesses, and much more. Sometimes with a self for me amazingly faster effect.

The possibilities to build up your places of power are unlimited. Here are some examples that I have built for myself:

I say my prayer in front of a beautiful little meditation cross that hangs in my study. I am there almost every day. Whenever I now consciously see my meditation cross, I think of my prayer and my wish-fulfillment. Of course, over time this happens subconsciously.

I bought a picture that hangs in the hallway and makes me feel wealth and prosperity. The picture hangs in such a way that I always have to see it when I walk through the hall. Every time it makes my heart beat faster when I see it and I feel the wealth.

I wear my Atlantis ring day and night wherever I am. It makes me feel success, happiness, and security. I am convinced that he has helped me very often and I am sincerely grateful for it.

On my window panes, I have symbols of strength, SRI YANTRA,

In every room. Symbols that for me radiate success, prosperity, and health in the whole room. Sometimes I stand in the middle of the room and feel this energy.

A brief explanation of the Sri-Yantra, by Michael Friedrich Vogt:

"Man is cosmic consciousness in an earthly-physical body. And with this awareness, we can let our impulses of consciousness ride on an energy wave that we can generate ourselves when we have learned this attitude of "unintentional" (not for influencing others but only for the growth of the whole) concentration to take as we can learn and experience it through the practice of meditation (self-hypnosis). The SRI-YANTRA can also generate these resonant energy waves with us and support us in building up these energy fields and sending them on a journey into the cosmic field of consciousness with our intentions. And we can surrender and love that opens this energy gate so that we can send our deepest impulses and intentions through the world and into this cosmic field of consciousness (universal consciousness). The SRI-YANTRA is an extraordinary tool for our energy and consciousness development and can enormously strengthen and accelerate our work on it, but not replace it. "

It fits! So why not use a symbol that is over 8,000 years old? The only important thing is that you believe in it and feel the energy and feelings of love.

This list is only an example. Look for your places of power or symbols, according to your taste and your wishes.

Finally, I would like to recommend one more thing to you. Don't just sit at home and wait for your wishes to come true. The more active you are, the faster your wishes will come true. So meet up with friends, join interest groups with interests that interest you, visit friends, acquaintances, and relatives, even those you haven't seen for a long time, get involved in a social group, and much more. So move actively and, through your willingness to cooperate, contribute directly or indirectly to fulfilling the wishes of others, the faster your wishes will come true.

11. Summary

Create the best conditions for your creative wish fulfillment by eliminating doubts and prejudices, transforming inhibiting beliefs into beneficial ones, and letting go of all superfluous negative thoughts and feelings.

Thought, body, and the physical world, feelings, depth consciousness, universal consciousness are connected and influence one another. They form a whole. Communication between them takes place through feelings.

Don't put your mind over your feelings. Your mind consists of half-knowledge, prejudice, and beliefs. Your feelings are the language of your soul and are true. They will show you the way to your happiness in this life. Therefore, do not judge them with your mind, for it is incapable of doing that. Use it to follow your feelings and make the right decisions.

Feelings are the universal language on all levels. If we understand the language of feelings and can communicate with them on all levels, then we can achieve anything we want, as long as it serves for further development.

Our deep consciousness is the bridge to the universal consciousness. Wishes are therefore brought into universal consciousness the fastest and most unambiguously via this bridge.

All forms of existence are designed for further development. Our goals and wishes have to be built into them to come true. All heart desires that serve this development and are communicated to the universal consciousness are supported by him.

Wishes become true if you recognize and use the right direct and indirect opportunities for cooperation that you get from the universal consciousness.

While proofreading, I noticed that I gave a relatively large number of examples in which relationship problems play a role. It's not a coincidence. Unresolved problems or unresolved lovesickness after a breakup often play a crucial role in the failure of wish fulfillment. If you are affected, I also recommend my little book "Lovesickness and Separation Pain." As an e-book for € 2.99

In this book, you have received all the information and guidance that can make you successful and happier. I am convinced of that. The only thing that can keep them from doing this is their patience and perseverance. Especially when working with their prejudices and beliefs. I know that from my practical experience with clients. Therefore, always keep in mind the enormous added value you will get if you work seriously on it. I wish you much success.

12. Book Recommendation

Book Description Traumata Part I

If you write about sex openly or speak publicly, most people feel bad about it. What is going on? Why are the strongest and most beautiful feelings so embarrassing for most of the world? You can give us a lot of joy and vitality. You don't talk about it because of

morality? What kind of morality and who made it? Do we have to follow this, even if we feel and think differently? What if our dreams and fantasies look completely different? How honest do we deal with it? Or to put it another way, why are we lying to ourselves? To adapt to so-called morality? Why has man been put into a sexual straitjacket and ashamed of his natural feelings? There is something wrong. More and more divorces, marriage violence, dramatic events due to jealousy and relationship stress, and much more show that something has to change fundamentally. The book answered these questions and made readers think. It can be the first step towards a new, happy future.

The book, Traumata of Mankind Part I Trauma Sex ", is even for Dr. Lutz Knoche a very special book. He has been dealing with this topic for years, which he also encountered more and more frequently in his practical work. He carried out a lot of spectacular research and targeted interviews and group discussions, which have found their way into this book.

ISBN 9783753442785
Is expected to be published in April 2021

Dr. Lutz Knoche
Video Bioenergetics massage

Stress and traumatic experiences also manifest themselves physically. Energy blockages arise.
Blockages that can weaken our body considerably.

The video shows you how you can remedy these disorders or significantly increase your general well-being. Suitable for private use or as a professional massage training.

It will be available on CD from May 2021. Duration approx. 90 minutes,

Price: € 29.95

Order and payment via PayPal

drlutzknoche@aol.com